Brain-Friendly
Study Strategies
Grades 2–8

W9-CPC-016

To Aunt Marie, whose one-room schoolhouse
first sparked my passion to teach,
to my parents who always supported me,
and to Jim, for his patience and loving support.

Janice Melichar-Utter

To my husband Richard
My best friend
My biggest advocate and supporter
My computer expert and problem solver
My sounding board for new ideas
I couldn't have written this book without your understanding,
patience, encouragement, love, and nurturing.

Amy Schwed

CURR LB 1601 .S38 2008
Schwed, Amy.
Brain-friendly study
 strategies, grades 2-8

Brain-Friendly Study Strategies

Grades 2–8

HOW TEACHERS CAN HELP STUDENTS LEARN

WITHDRAWN

CURRICULUM MATERIALS
BALDWIN WALLACE UNIVERSITY

AMY SCHWED

JANICE MELICHAR-UTTER

CORWIN PRESS
A SAGE Publications Company
Thousand Oaks, CA 91320

Copyright © 2008 by Corwin Press

All rights reserved. When forms and sample documents are included, their use is authorized only by educators, local school sites, and/or noncommercial or nonprofit entities that have purchased the book. Except for that usage, no part of this book may be reproduced or utilized in any form or by any means, electronic or mechanical, including photocopying, recording, or by any information storage and retrieval system, without permission in writing from the publisher.

For information:

Corwin Press, Inc.
A SAGE Company
2455 Teller Road
Thousand Oaks, California 91320
www.corwinpress.com

SAGE Ltd.
1 Oliver's Yard
55 City Road
London, EC1Y 1SP
United Kingdom

SAGE India Pvt. Ltd.
B 1/I 1 Mohan Cooperative
Industrial Area
Mathura Road, New Delhi 110 044
India

SAGE Asia-Pacific Pte. Ltd.
33 Pekin Street #02-01
Far East Square
Singapore 048763

Printed in the United States of America

Library of Congress Cataloging-in-Publication Data
Schwed, Amy.
Brain-friendly study strategies, grades 2-8 : how teachers can help students learn / Amy Schwed and Janice Melichar-Utter.
    p. cm.
Includes bibliographical references.
ISBN 978-1-4129-6105-9 (cloth)
ISBN 978-1-4129-4251-5 (pbk.)
    1. Study skills—Study and teaching (Elementary) 2. Study skills—Study and teaching (Middle school) 3. Brain. I. Melichar-Utter, Janice. II. Title.

LB1601.S38 2008
372.13028'1—dc22

2007040298

This book is printed on acid-free paper.

07 08 09 10 11 10 9 8 7 6 5 4 3 2 1

Acquisitions Editor: Faye Zucker
Managing Editor: Carol Chambers Collins
Editorial Assistants: Gem Rabanera, Brett Ory
Production Editor: Appingo Publishing Services
Cover Designer: Monique Hahn
Graphic Designer: Lisa Miller

Contents

**A Guide to Study Strategy Activities in the Chapters,
with Corresponding Grade Levels**

A Guide to Study Strategy Activities in the Chapters, with Corresponding Grade Levels

A Guide to Study Strategy Activities in the Chapters, with Corresponding Grade Levels

Acknowledgments

We were motivated by exciting new ideas gleaned from workshops and books by master teachers and researchers. To Madeline Hunter, Pat Wolfe, Howard Gardner, Lisa Sambora, Carolyn Chapman, Rita Dunn, Gail Dusa, Tom Armstrong, David Lazear, David Sousa, Robin Fogarty, Eric Jensen, and Marilee Sprenger we are greatly indebted. These individuals strongly influenced our teaching. Some of our strategies were adapted from these masters. Others were developed as we strived to meet student needs, and still others were born through the synergism of working with colleagues. All are tried and true. As our understanding of how the brain learns increased, so did our ability to teach so students learned more efficiently.

We are grateful to our colleagues in the Carmel Central School District, Carmel, New York, especially to the dedicated teachers at George Fischer Middle School who provided synergy, patience, and encouragement. Special thanks are given to Cinthia Goepfrich, Margaret Fennessy, Carol Martoccia, Maureen Stoll, Keith Tucci, and Charlotte Woodward for putting up with some of our crazy ideas as well as contributing to activities in this book. Additionally, we appreciate W. Jim Welling and Dr. Marilyn Brannigan—administrators who supported and provided freedom to experiment.

We thank the wonderful teachers in the Arlington Central School District, Arlington, New York, who attended our workshops and provided invaluable feedback, inspiring us to write this book. The following graduate students at State University of New York at New Paltz, New York, graciously shared their ideas: Jennifer Capozzi, Kathleen Collin, Joann Gradzki, Leigh Flood-Legare, Melissa Rogers, Kelli Trevorah, Jodi Vines, and Lilah Weiss.

We appreciate Amy's brother, Bruce Wasserman, whose computer graphics creatively illustrate this book. We are indebted to him for his willingness to tackle the illustrations and make countless revisions until they were "just right."

Many thanks go to a dear friend, Vicki Greenberg, who proofread the first few chapters and provided insightful feedback and encouragement.

We value our reviewer's guidance helping us clarify our focus; we appreciate the professional input. Thank you!

Most important of all, we thank all the students we have had the pleasure of knowing. Each one came to us with vastly different abilities and learning styles and challenged us to seek new ways to teach. They became our teachers and we learned from each other.

We are indebted to our husbands who put up with our writing preoccupation and harried schedules. They encouraged us to attend conferences, present workshops, and were there whenever we needed a listening ear. Through it all, they remain our strongest supporters. All our love!

Corwin Press gratefully acknowledges the contributions of the following reviewers:

Patricia DeLessio
Professor of English and Reading
Dutchess Community College

Marilee Sprenger
Adjunct Professor of brain-based teaching, learning and memory, and
    differentiation
Aurora University, IL
Peoria, IL

Reva Cowan
Associate Professor of Education
Mount Saint Mary College
Newburgh, NY

Barbara J. Donegan
Assistant Superintendent for PPS
Arlington Central School District
Poughkeepsie, NY

Winifred Montgomery
Chair and Associate Professor
Department of Elementary Education
State University of New York at New Paltz
New Paltz, NY

Barbara Chorzempa
Assistant Professor
Department of Elementary Education
State University of New York at New Paltz
New Paltz, NY

About the Authors

Amy Schwed is an adjunct professor at the State University of New York at New Paltz. During the past eleven years, she has developed courses in how to teach reading/language arts at both primary and intermediate levels, as well as children's literature and differentiated instruction classes, and supervised student teachers. In addition, she created and taught a graduate course, "Integrating Study Skills and Multiple Intelligences." That course, combined with a shortened version developed for inservice teacher training, was the genesis of *Brain-Friendly Study Strategies* and has undergone continual growth and change.

Her professional background includes thirty-one years as a public school educator in kindergarten through eighth grade; eleven years as a college professor; reading teacher, and consultant in elementary, middle school, and junior highs; teacher of middle school gifted and talented students; New York State "Newspapers in Education" turn-key trainer; staff development and inservice teacher trainer for many school districts; and workshop presenter for parent education training. In addition to being a teacher trainer, she has been a repeat presenter at many professional conferences, including the International Reading Association, the New York State Reading Association, local reading councils, and other state conferences. She developed and conducted a districtwide Young Author's Conference for several years. She has been a returning guest lecturer at Vassar College and Manhattanville College.

Since beginning research to design the integrated study skills graduate course, she has become actively involved in discovering as much about how the brain learns as possible. This has become an ongoing, fascinating educational process, exciting and informing her current teaching. That research broadened the scope of brain-friendly study strategies well beyond multiple intelligences. She loves being a teacher of current and future teachers! She may be reached at amyschwed@optonline.net.

Janice Melichar-Utter has worked with students at all levels from preschool to college during her thirty-four years in education. She was an adjunct professor at Mount Saint Mary College teaching Foundations of Literacy. Presently, Jan tutors women recovering from substance abuse. Working as a reading specialist for eighteen years, primarily at the middle school level, Jan learned to adapt strategies to meet the challenges of learning disabled and gifted readers. In the social studies classroom, she was passionate about developing brain-friendly study strategies and memory techniques to bring success to all students. Guiding students to understand how they learned became paramount to covering curriculum.

Jan presents teacher workshops on a variety of topics throughout the Hudson Valley, including the New York State Reading Association Conferences, Mid-Hudson Reading Council Fall Conferences, the IRA Convention in Toronto, Canada and was a guest lecturer at Vassar College for over twenty years. As readability editor and consultant for Scholastic-Grolier, she involved her middle school students in focus groups to evaluate books. She is a member of professional organization such as ASCD, MHRC, Delta Kappa Gamma, and APCE.

Currently, Jan is using her educational background for work in Christian ministry. She and her husband Jim, an ecology professor, live in the Hudson Valley of New York and share five children and four grandchildren in their combined family.

Jan can be reached at mrsjmutter98@aol.com.

Introduction

During the last decade of our tenure in public education, we challenged ourselves to incorporate recent brain research—first into daily teaching activities, and then, specifically focusing on teaching study skills. We realized students needed to be taught to study and this could not be accomplished in an isolated study skills unit. Long-term memory increases if students are given step-by-step guidance in studying within each content area, which is why we strongly feel study skill lessons must be integrated.

We believe the more teachers understand the human brain, the better prepared they are to influence learners. A simple diagram from Dr. Pat Wolfe showing how the brain learns was the first influential spark, motivating us to integrate brain-friendly strategies and study skills. It made us realize the road to long-term memory is a painful trek for some students who may be journeying down the wrong path. Finding the right strategy brings joy to the journey and shortens the road to their final destination.

Each September parents would come to school to learn about curriculum. Once the curriculum was shared, we would explain that there would be times when study skills might be stressed more than content. Heads always nodded in agreement. Content facts can be quickly found in texts, reference books, or on the Internet; however, a variety of study techniques need to be modeled, then ingrained, and made personal, since we all learn in different ways. We became passionate about this as we saw students succeed and former students return to share how they continually used the study skills they had learned.

We seized opportunities to share our concept of integrating study skills and brain research with our colleagues. This led to the development of a graduate education course, then teaching inservice courses for teachers and conducting courses for parents in the Arlington, New York, school district. It is the positive feedback and encouragement from graduate students at the State University of New York at New Paltz, as well as the veteran teachers in Arlington telling us that "You just have to put all these great ideas into a book," which motivated us to undertake writing this book. To the best of our knowledge, there is no such book currently on the market. There are many that deal with brain research, others that promote study skills, but none that integrate both. Our book fills this niche!

We love energizing teachers who will, in turn, motivate and guide their students in developing lifelong study skills using all of their learning strengths in the most brain-friendly ways. Learning is a never-ending journey, traveling many different and unique pathways.

This "teacher-friendly" book presents "brain-friendly" study strategies valuable to educators in all areas and at a wide range of levels. No prerequisite knowledge is required as we provide background information.

Myriad practical, ready-to-use ideas, applying study strategies to the unique learning ability/style of each student, usable in all contents areas and levels, are the major strengths of this book. The ideas shared are viable for teaching in primary grades through adult learners, for special education and special area teachers, and even for school psychologists! Additionally, parents will find this book valuable as they work with their children.

The first three chapters provide easy to grasp background on how the brain and memory work and show how different modalities affect learning. Chapter 4 discusses the physical and emotional needs of a healthy brain. The next six chapters provide study strategies differentiated for each learner's strengths enabling teachers and parents to match students with study techniques that are brain compatible. The final two chapters provide time management strategies and metacognitive activities, including a rubric to self-evaluate study. Our approaches are fun and highly successful.

—Amy Schwed and Janice Melichar-Utter

Introducing the Brain: Hooking Into Your Memory

Overview

PROCESS VERSUS CONTENT

Think with us for a moment. Jot down all the things you teach your students that **can't** be found on the Internet or in reference materials such as an encyclopedia, atlas, or almanac, as well as things written in textbooks.

_____

_____

_____

_____

Now categorize them by putting a check next to each item that is a process or strategy. What do you notice? Did you check off classroom management tips? Were there any "getting along with your peers" ideas? Perhaps you listed how to take notes, organize a binder, use the library, or even how to put a heading on a paper. Or maybe ways to work in a cooperative learning group. And you might have included some study skills.

Generally, you would **not** have included any content concepts or facts, since they are easily located in texts and references. We recognize that process trumps content—even in our curricula-driven schools—since process is lifelong learning.

We think of study skills as the effective use of appropriate techniques for completing a learning task, which is any activity that is designed to help students achieve an instructional objective. Here are some typical school learning tasks:

- Managing time, materials, yourself
- Listening and taking notes in class
- Answering teacher questions and participating in class activities
- Reading textbooks and other materials
- Writing papers
- Preparing for taking tests

As students study for tests, they are stimulated to engage in new learning and to consolidate what they have already learned by **reorganizing** it for easy retrieval. New state tests integrate study skill and content information.

Teachers need to become aware of the importance of *process* in learning. The more teachers lead students to reflect on **how** they process information into long-term memory, the more students will become efficient learners. Students will profit from teachers who ask the following questions:

How did you learn that?
What tricks did you use?

Since students can't *make meaning* and *process meaning* at the same time (Lyle, 2006), provide reflection time to help students become aware of each step in their learning process. As awareness is gained, guide students to think about other ways to apply the techniques. Initially, doing this is time consuming, but the rewards are great and will "pay back" the time in the future.

A student who has good study skills can successfully carry out any learning task. A student with poor study skills may carry out the same learning task, but may use inappropriate techniques in an ineffective manner. This student's work requires more time and produces poorer results because retrieval is slower or information is not totally secured in long-term memory. By giving students a wide variety of study skills, they can choose the ones that work for them. It is our goal that each student will develop study processes or strategies that will last for a lifetime and be adaptable to anything that the student must remember. We believe that the most opportune time to establish these study techniques is during grades two to six, with reinforcement in grades seven and up. And keep in mind that all learning involves the transfer of previous experiences and prior knowledge (Lyle, 2006).

STUDY SKILLS CANNOT BE TAUGHT IN ISOLATION

Our experience shows us **study skills cannot be taught in isolation**. When taught as an add-on class, transfer is unlikely. The efficacy—not to mention everyone's time—is lost. We have learned how much *all* **students need step-by-step guidance in learning how to study**. Infusing study skills into any curriculum helps students connect the learning into long-term memory. When teaching any content area, specifically introduce one new study skill with each unit throughout the year. Although teachers feel a strong tendency to get as many study skills into the hands and minds of students as soon as possible, be sure to give enough classroom practice time for each skill to allow it to "sink in." We feel that the study skills are more important for lifelong learning in our fast-paced, technological world than curriculum content is. In fact, we began to feel the step-by-step instruction of study strategies—although time consuming—was the *most* important thing we were giving our students.

At our parent-teacher curriculum meeting, we explained the content of the curriculum and then told parents that the subject matter was secondary to the study strategies taught along with the content; heads often nodded in agreement. This goes along with an old proverb: "Give a man a fish and he will eat for a day. Teach him how to fish and he will eat for a lifetime." We want students who will know how to study **for a lifetime**.

KNOW YOUR BRAIN

At this point, we'd like to present some background information on how the brain functions. Dr. Daniel Amen (2005, introduction) has told us, "The brain is involved in everything you do. How you think, how you feel, how you act, and how well you get along with people has to do with the moment-by-moment functioning of your brain" (p. xiii).

Understanding Amen's message is essential to effective teaching. As you become aware of how *you* learn, you will be better able to increase student learning. First, actively teach students *how* they learn, using Figure 1.1. As students understand learning, they will increase both their understanding and their ability to use new information. You will discover better ways to structure a variety of classroom activities. Our entire educational system profits as we design curriculum to be brain friendly, especially since the brain resists meaninglessness.

Patricia Wolfe (1991) stated that "the human brain is a **three pound universe.** You have at least 10 billion nerve cells in your brain . . . perhaps 100 billion. Each of these nerve cells makes between 5,000 and 50,000 contacts with other nerve cells . . . so, using a very conservative estimate (10 billion cells $\times$ 10,000 contacts) you end up with **100 TRILLION** connections" Wolfe, P. (p.1) This is enough space to store a lifetime of learning—and each brain is unique.

Figure 1.1 Know Your Brain

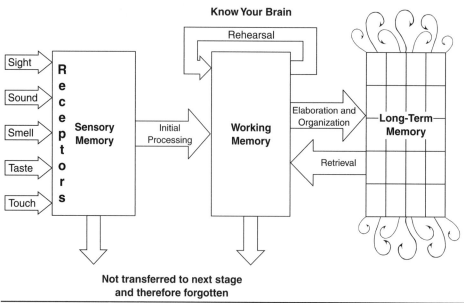

SOURCE: adapted from Wolfe (2001)

Looking at Figure 1.1, notice that five sensory receptors receive information: sight, sound, smell, taste, and touch. The brain is constantly scanning the environment for stimuli that enters through sensory memory. Simultaneously, enormous amounts of sensory input bombard the brain, which unconsciously sifts and sorts out unimportant items. If there are no meaningful connections, the duration of visual information can be measured in milliseconds, but auditory signals may last up to twenty seconds. Wolfe compared the brain to a sieve, since as much as 99 percent of irrelevant sensory information is discarded almost immediately upon entering the brain. In this process, ". . .the brain checks the existing neural network of information to see if the new information is something that activates a previously stored neural network" (Wolfe, 2001, p. 81). Thus, our perception and meaning are influenced by the information we have stored in our brain. Nothing is retained without a connection to prior knowledge. The more you know, the easier it is to learn!

If new information is meaningful or stirs an emotion, the brain will attend to it. When the brain is prepared—put on alert—by activating background information, then data deemed important after this initial processing will be moved into short-term memory. This is the **working brain**—metacognition happens here! It's where we "think about thinking." Short-term memory is shorter than you think! If we do not connect or process information in some meaningful way, new ideas or facts will only be kept for fifteen to twenty seconds! There are times students can hold information in short-term memory long enough to pass a test. Then, with a sigh of relief, they drop it! Bet we've all done that! However, that's not our goal.

When we experience something new, the brain looks for an existing circuit or network into which the new information will fit. This is why it is so important to activate background knowledge and prepare the brain to make a connection between new learning and previously established information. "Deep understanding is acquired when students get a feeling for the meaning of an idea which involves learning about a topic in an in-depth manner. The teacher makes connections to prior knowledge, and thus creates a solid neural network highway" (Connell, 2005, p. 112). Where prior knowledge and experience do not exist, the teacher needs to provide it before teaching new material (Tileston, 2004). Information drops out if no "hook" is established. When background knowledge prepares the brain, it is more likely that a connection will be made and new ideas will be secured. "Learning is all about making connections" (Connell, 2005, p. 16; see also Figure 1.2).

Figure 1.2

Ways to Activate Background Knowledge
AND
"Wake Up the Brain"

- As a class, list student contributions of what they know about any topic. Do in "whip-around" style.
  Remember, sharing promotes learning.
- Use a KWL format.*
- Create a web/mind map of known ideas.
- Read a topic related poem.
- Share a related experience.
- Discuss a "What would I do if . . ."
- Read and discuss a short story related to the topic.
- Do a read aloud.
- Do an anticipation guide with key points (Wormeli, 2005, p. 97–99). *See Human Continuum, Chapter 7.*
- In a text, survey by reading pictures, charts, maps, and their captions.
- Predict what might be encountered in the materials.
- Ask for a variety of ways a problem may be solved. How would *you* solve it?
- Do a "quick write."**
- Use video clips or quality educational television shows to prompt discussion.
- Present a physical object that stimulates topic discussion.
- Do a vocabulary splash. Put words on tag board with magnets on the back so words can then be moved into categories.

---

*A *KWL* chart is a three-column chart used to both activate background knowledge and motivate students. In the first column, *K*, students brainstorm and list everything they *Know* about the topic being discussed. The second column, *W*, is where we note what students *Want* to know or *Wonder* about. (This is where teachers can add their "two cents" and include things they feel must be emphasized.)

These are both filled in before beginning a new topic or text. The last column, *L*, lists what students have *Learned* and is filled in when the unit or text is completed. **A *quick write* allows students to generate and explore relationships among ideas, make connections, and reflect on learning. Teachers direct students to write for five or ten minutes on the topic to be studied. Writing is impromptu and nonstructured and is used as a thinking tool because the focus is on content, with no emphasis on mechanics. Young children can draw pictures and add labels. When completed, students share their quick writes in small groups or with the whole class.

REHEARSAL

Notice how rehearsal is wrapped around working memory in Figure 1.1. Rehearsal is imprinting to hold ideas in the short-term memory long enough to move the concept into long-term memory. Some children can do this in one or two repetitions; however, most usually need many more. In fact, many students need as much as twenty-four to twenty-eight reviews, spaced over a three-week period, to set information into long-term memory (Sprenger, 2006). We like to consider rehearsal "playing with new learning." There are two types of rehearsal: rote rehearsal and elaborative rehearsal. Rote rehearsal is the deliberate, continuous repetition of material in the same form in which it entered short-term memory. Although memorizing is not an efficient way to learn, there are times when it is appropriate such as when learning times tables. Elaborative rehearsal involves elaborating or integrating information, giving it meaning—creating chunks of reminders, such as noticing the relationships of numbers in the nine times table, which is why students have no trouble learning those facts. Rehearsal is necessary to achieve long-term memory and get students involved with new ideas.

Figure 1.3 Rehearsal

Rehearsal Builds Muscle Memory
By **maintaining** information in short-term memory
and
By **transferring** information to long-term memory

Two types of rehearsal:

Rote Rehearsal	*Elaborative Rehearsal*
Deliberate, continuous repetition of material in the same form in which it entered short-term memory	Elaborating or integrating information with some kind of meaning—creating chunks of reminders

- Drill with multiplication/ division facts
- Recitation of dates in history
- Repeated writing of spelling words
- Memorization of Periodic Table

- Talk about new learning
- Read about new learning
- See a movie related to lesson
- Translate information into symbols, either concrete or abstract
- Make a crossword puzzle that utilizes new terms and concepts
- Draw something related to lesson
- Discuss new learning in small groups
- Depict new learning through a mind map
- Make up related rhymes and jingles
- Associate physical movements with new learning
- Create and play games with new learning
- Use role-plays and simulations with new learning
- Tell or write stories or poems with new information
- Incorporate humor and laughter with new learning

The brain LOVES elaborative rehearsal!

The elaboration and organization of new ideas is what moves learning into long-term memory. Once again, look at Figure 1.1. Notice that long-term memory is divided into cubbyholes and has many hooks. These cubbies and hooks contain information forming the schemata, or framework, to which new knowledge is attached. The more you know, the easier it is to add learning, since there are more hooks, pegs, or cubbies to which the new information can be attached. It is virtually impossible to learn something *totally* new, as there is no schema to "hook" into!

Long-term memory has no limits. Once a fact or concept is in long-term memory, it stays there. Retrieval, however, is the big challenge! The older one gets, the harder it is to **access** what is known, since so much more is known. We may have to ask, "What cubby did I file that under?" "How did I connect that?" "When or where did I learn that?"

MEMORY HIGHWAYS

All roads lead to long-term memory. Let's take a look at Figure 1.4, which presents the two types of long-term memory: explicit memory (declarative and verbal) and implicit memory (nondeclarative and nonverbal).

Figure 1.4 Roads to Long-Term Memory

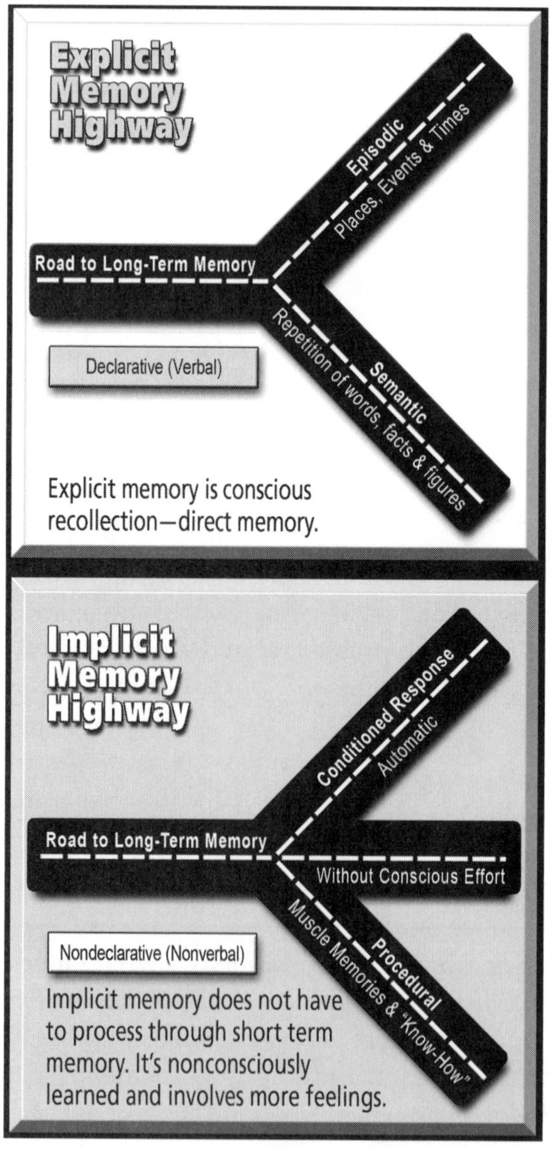

Illustration by Bruce Wasserman

Marilee Sprenger (2003, p. 131) shared an acronym telling how memory **CREEPS** down different highways into long-term memory.

CR is for **C**onditioned **R**esponse

E is for **E**motional

E is for **E**pisodic

P is for **P**rocedural

S is for **S**emantic

While we work with students, our goal is to guide them in discovering which memory highway works best for each subject. As people store memory using various paths, they also retrieve memories differently, depending on the cues.

Have you ever left a room to get something, only to arrive without remembering what you came for? We call that "destinesia" (destination amnesia), and it ties into retrieval of information. "What am I here for?" you ask yourself. Retrieval is not always easy! "Having a strong memory in storage does not guarantee that you will later retrieve the memory successfully" (Squire & Kandel, as cited in Sprenger, 2005, p. 140).

The retrieval process requires us to move through a series of steps (connections) before we can find information. Key to retrieval is organization. Remembering major concepts in categories will trigger supporting details. We can automatically retrieve some information, like driving, keyboarding, decoding, and other such highly repetitive processes. **Study skills are all about meaningful elaboration in rehearsal that makes new learning retrievable**.

When working with students, one cannot neglect the role of emotions on learning. Experts note that students are more likely to attend to and remember information if it has meaning to the student and contains an *emotional* "hook." The emotional center of our brains provides us with the feeling of what is real, true, and important. This strongly influences what we pay attention to. Under stress, the brain "downshifts," narrowing our perceptual field, and we lose much of our capacity for rational and creative thought. For example, when one feels embarrassed, scared, or threatened, the ability to learn decreases. A nonthreatening, safe environment enables the brain to operate most efficiently. However, an optimal level of emotion is necessary for learning to occur. Positive energy or heightened curiosity both hold the student's attention and keep the student's focus on learning. The opposite is also true; emotion can be a double-edged sword (Wolfe, 2001).

No emotion = no learning!   Fun is preferable to fear!

FACTORS INFLUENCING ATTENTION

Anything capturing students' attention and getting their minds engaged has the potential to produce learning. So what factors influence attention?

- Students must know why they **"need"** to learn something or how it will have **meaning** in their lives.
- Any **novel** approach will grab attention: use music, wear costumes, or move in a manner different from your normal way. "Unfamiliar activities are the brain's best friend" (Scheibel, as cited in Jensen, 2000, p. 154).
- **Cognitive dissonance** (saying the opposite of what you mean) catches student attention. For example, saying, "Don't listen to this!" automatically prompts students to pay attention. Curiosity is piqued.
- We need to communicate high, clear **expectations**; then students can focus on the goal.
- **Intensify the stimuli**. For example, use different voice inflections and volume, or change the physical layout of the room.
- Students consider **humor** one of the most important teacher traits. "The brain retains information at a 35 percent to 45 percent higher rate through humor" (Redenback, 2003, p. 3). Therefore humor promotes learning!
- Finally, create positive **emotion**. Your passion for what you are teaching will draw students to love what they are learning.

Teachers frequently say, "That student isn't paying attention." This isn't true. The brain is **always** paying attention to something; what we're really saying is that the student is not paying attention to what *we* think is important. The brain needs "down" time to process new information. Teachers need to present information in smaller chunks, with time for rehearsal provided immediately following instruction. Alternate instruction and rehearsal. Plan time for students to reflect on what they have just learned by writing in journals; sharing information with a partner; or reviewing the material by drawing, illustrating, or otherwise creating visual representations of it (D'Arcangelo, 2006).

The human brain is truly awesome! It is forever changing. Information is processed as billions of neurons "talk" to each other to make new connections that retain new learning. This is ultimately what learning is all about. The longer we have taught and the more we have learned about the brain, the more fascinating it has been to watch the variety of ways in which students learn.

"Memories must be rehearsed in multiple ways to store them in many areas of the brain."

—Sprenger

"I forget what I was taught. I only remember what I have learned."

—Patrick White

"Retrieved memories are the only evidence we have of learning."

—Sprenger

"It's not how much you know about the brain that matters, it's how much you apply."

—Jensen

"The brain that does the work is the brain that learns!"

—Wolfe

SUMMARY OF KEY CONCEPTS IN THIS CHAPTER

- The learning *process* is more important than the content mastered.
- Step-by-step study skills need to be imbedded within curriculum; they cannot be taught in isolation.
- Understanding how the brain processes information increases learning efficiency.
- Learning is all about making connections.
- Activating background knowledge is key to getting the brain's attention and retaining new learning.
- Rehearsal is the conveyer belt to move information into long-term memory.
- Long-term memory CREEPS down memory highways.
- Information is more likely to be attended to and remembered if it has meaning to the student and contains an "emotional hook."
- Many factors work to capture students' attention, such as meaningfulness, novelty, cognitive dissonance, high expectations, intensified stimuli, humor, and positive emotions.

e

2

Learning What Works for You

Modalities and Styles Awareness

In an optimal learning environment, both instructors and students would be aware of how they learn and what factors affect their learning. How do you learn best? _____
What factors affect your learning? _____

Knowing this empowers both students and teachers. Many different sources report that students learn best when matched with teachers who share the same learning style. Therefore, it is important for both students and teachers to be conscious of their strongest learning modality. An individual's learning style is the same **regardless of the subject area**!

HOW WE LEARN

Although we have five sensory receptors, schools traditionally focus on three modalities:

1. Visual

2. Auditory

3. Kinesthetic

Modalities refers to the modes or senses through which people *take in* and *process* information. A modality is more than simply labeling a person visual, auditory, or kinesthetic.

Visual

Two types of **visual** learners exist: **picture** learners and **print** learners. *Picture* learners enjoy materials including charts, graphs, designs, forms, layouts, maps, objects, drawings, movies, and dramatic performances. They translate all types of incoming information into pictures before processing, memorizing, or acting on anything. *Print* learners think in words. They see words in their minds when they are listening, memorizing, recalling, and thinking. When asked to spell a word, these learners say, "Let me write it down to see how it looks." They convert pictures into words. They need to read and write in order to efficiently process information. Highlighting in different colors is a great strategy for this type of learner, as is making notes and diagrams in the margins.

Auditory

Auditory factors encompasses many things: noise, music, songs, lectures, verbal explanations, taped information, stories told aloud, conversations, and the sound of one's own voice. Some auditory learners need to talk to be able to process information. They need to actually *say* the words, not simply *hear* someone else say them. Reading instructions aloud to oneself has worked wonders for those individuals who have trouble understanding written directions. These students will also increase their reading comprehension as they hear themselves read difficult passages aloud. We have had great success using a **"phonics phone"** with this type of youngster.

Phonics phones are very easy to make using PVC pipe and elbows (see Appendix for directions), or they can be purchased through the Crystal Springs catalog for a very reasonable price. Their Web site is www.crystalsprings.com.

Additional uses include the following:

- Allow the auditory learners to use their phonics phone when taking a test, so they can read the test aloud and hear themselves without disturbing other students.
- Before asking students to do oral reading, let them practice with their phone first.
- When buddy reading with children, partners can use the phone by just turning one piece of the elbow toward the second student.

Warn your students that they must use **whisper voices** (two-inch voices) when they use the phones, as it is truly astounding how it amplifies the voice. What amazing miracles the phones provide for auditory learners!

Figure 2.1   Phonics Phone

Illustration by Bruce Wasserman

Kinesthetic

The third learning modality is **kinesthetic/tactile**, meaning the use of touch and movement in learning. It is the most difficult modality to understand. Learners who use this modality receive information more efficiently when they are able to touch things and move around; they may be the students who tap their feet, doodle, color, touch new things, and so forth. They may not appear to be paying attention, but can repeat what was said! These students benefit from "pointing" when they read, "using fingers" to add, and so forth. Some *hands-on learners* process best through activities, such as constructing, assembling, taking things apart, working with textured materials, and manipulating objects. Others are *whole-body learners* who need to act out, walk around, play, exercise, build, give live demonstrations, and use whole-body movements, thereby building muscle memory. *Sketching learners* learn through drawing, coloring, and doodling. *Writing learners* need the kinesthetic activity of actually writing to assist their learning. These students choose to write spelling words, foreign language vocabulary, math facts, or scientific formulas many times, just so they can remember them—*not because the teacher gave that assignment.*

Some studies show that kinesthetic/tactile is the strongest modality, followed by visual, and then the auditory modality. We are all kinesthetic learners, however, which means that our memories will increase as objects are touched and handled. Thus, experiments, real-life experiences, excursions, movement, and art are extremely beneficial to the memory process for every learner.

LEARNING STYLES INVENTORY

Jot down what you think is your strongest learning modality.

_____

Take a few minutes to complete the Learning Styles Cognitive Preference Inventory (Figure 2.2) that follows. It will help you begin to explore which strategies work best for you. Was your prediction accurate? This inventory will provide you and your students with an opportunity to discover the learning modality strengths of each individual and which strategies work best for each person. Ask students to predict their learning modalities by writing their prediction on the top of the inventory before they begin. After the assessment is completed, see if the students' self-predictions were correct. If this task uncovers new strength awareness, encourage students to try different strategies to capitalize on these strengths.

Figure 2.2   Learning Styles Cognitive Preference Inventory

Learning Styles Cognitive Preference Inventory

Circle the option (V, A, or K) that best relates to you most of the time. You may choose more than one option. Your first reaction is usually the best response.

1. I "take in" new information best when:
    V - I can see information in picture or diagram form.
    A - someone talks or explains to me.
    K - I can get hands-on experience.

2. When I am giving directions, I usually:
    V - draw a map.
    A - tell them how to get there.
    K - take the person and show them the way.

3. I remember directions best when:
    V - someone gives landmarks to guide me.
    A - I have oral directions and repeat them aloud.
    K - I have been taken through the route once.

4. When I am not sure how to spell a word, I often:
    V - see the word in my mind and "see" how to spell it.
    A - sound the word out in my mind or aloud.
    K - write down different versions of the spelling.

(continued)

Figure 2.2 (continued)

5. To remember and recall an event, I would want to:
    V - see pictures or read a description.
    A - tell it aloud to someone.
    K - replay it through movement—acting, pantomime, or drill.

6. I seem to remember objects better if:
    V - I can see a picture, a pattern.
    A - I create jingles or rhymes.
    K - I have touched or worked with them.

7. When using a new piece of equipment, i.e., computer or camera, I would:
    V - read the directions or watch someone do it.
    A - ask someone to "talk" me through it.
    K - jump right in and figure it out.

8. I enjoy:
    V - making or viewing slides and photographs.
    A - reciting or writing poetry.
    K - working with my hands repairing and building things.

9. I prefer to find out about something new by:
    V - reading about it.
    A - talking about it.
    K - doing it.

10. I prefer a teacher who uses:
    V - charts, diagrams, and overheads.
    A - discussion and guest speakers.
    K - field trips and practical sessions.

Visual _____ (Prefer to take in information by seeing and reading)

Auditory _____ (Prefer to take in information by listening and talking)

Kinesthetic _____ (Prefer to take in information by doing and practicing)

The highest score represents your greatest strength.
If scores are tied, you may operate equally well in two or three areas.

It is important to remember that we utilize all three modalities.

SOURCE: Chernin (2004) http://www.georgebrown.ca/saffairs/stusucc/learningstyles.aspx. Permission granted.

Did any of your students have dual strengths? What does that mean? It means they have two comfortable ways to receive, process, and disperse new information. There are students who have an even balance of all three styles, but their preferences affect the order in which they best take in information and enhance their learning and mastery. Guide students to study using their strongest mode and provide opportunities to strengthen the weakest modality. "Understanding your cognitive preferences means that you can ask for information and seek opportunities that will ensure optimum mastery/learning" (Chernin, 2004). Figure 2.3 lists a variety of strategies accessing all modalities that students can use to study.

Provide each student with a copy of this diagram and encourage him or her to try several new strategies.

Figure 2.3

V-A-K Study Strategies

Visual Study Strategies

- use guided imagery
- take notes
- use color codes
- use charts, graphs, maps, timelines
- organize through mind maps
- create a photo journal

- form mental pictures to increase understanding
- use "cue" words
- use flash cards—sometimes with picture clues
- draw/use drawings
- use mnemonics, acrostics, and acronyms
- design an ad or poster

Auditory Study Strategies

- use tapes
- read material aloud
- repeat things orally
- use mnemonics and lyrics
- engage in a debate
- give a speech

- make up rhymes, poems songs, jingles, stories, and raps
- discuss with others/pretend to teach a lesson
- listen to oral directions
- present a newscast
- use a phonics phone

Kinesthetic Study Strategies

- pace/walk when studying
- practice with repeated motions
- take notes
- write on surfaces with finger or in the air with an elbow or foot
- use mnemonics, rhymes, poems, and lyrics

- role-play with props
- dance out ideas
- write lists repeatedly
- associate feelings with concept/information
- create a game
- use manipulatives

We need to train students to transfer information they must learn into their brain's most comfortable learning modality. Studying with visual, auditory, and kinesthetic modalities makes learning more efficient and permanent, as more hooks connect into long-term memory. In addition, people achieve higher-level reasoning skills when they learn through their strongest modality. Traditional schools primarily teach to the auditory and visual learners, thus shortchanging kinesthetic/tactile learners. By doing so, they also shortchange other learners, since lessons that incorporate **movement** and **doing** are valuable for everyone. The use of all three modalities also increases retrieval of information. Wolfe (1998) stated, "The more modalities we use to store the information or experience, the more pathways we have available to access it" (p. 64).

EMPOWERING LEARNING

Teachers need to integrate visual, auditory, and kinesthetic methods in order to reach learners who learn through different modalities. In the late 1960s, William Glasser popularized this point with the following concept:

WE LEARN
10% of what we read
20% of what we hear
30% of what we see
50% of what we both see and hear
70% of what is discussed with others
80% of what we experience personally
95% of what we TEACH to someone else

As we researched this quote, however, we discovered some shocking information. Dr. Glasser has been credited with "We Learn," but he "simply referred to it based on his readings. He says he pretty much agrees with it, but is not the originator" (William Glasser Institute, n.d.). Continued research unearthed Edgar Dales's (1946, as cited in, Work-Learning Research, 2006) "Cone of Experience" theory, which states that, after two weeks, we tend to remember

10% of what we read
20% of what we hear
30% of what we see
50% of what we hear and see
70% of what we say
90% of what we both say and do

Further investigation on this topic discovered a 1967 article by D.G. Treichler (as cited in Work-Learning Research, 2006) that discusses these percentages. Treichler's numbers appear to have been heavily influenced by Dale's 1946 "Cone of Experience" (Hornswaggled, n.d.). Believe it or not, people at Work-Learning Research, explained, "Although we at Work-Learning Research have not concluded our investigation of this hoax, it appears that those percentages, were probably generated by an employee of Mobil Oil Company in 1967 writing in the magazine *Film and Audio-Visual Communications*. Treichler didn't cite any research, but our field has unfortunately accepted his/her percentages ever since." Yet, going back to Dale, he warned his readers not to take the model too literally. Kinnamon (2002, as cited in Work-Learning Research, 2006) found that "Treichler's percentages have been modified in many ways. . . . Some people changed the relative percentages. Some have added categories to make their point."

If you stop to think about the above data, we can ultimately trace the "We Learn" back to an old Chinese proverb:

I hear and I forget;
I see and I remember;
I do and I understand.

Despite the lack of sound research we have consciously decided to include the Glasser and Dale information in this book since they have had a profound, positive, and far-reaching impact on education. From them, we have learned to

- Not rely on lecture alone;
- Encourage students to read aloud to increase comprehension;
- Use visual aids, such as white board, overhead, and PowerPoint to support auditory input;
- Use small group interactions, allowing students to solve problems and discuss issues;
- Use journaling assignments and essay questions to reflect on and personalize curriculum;
- Have students teach each other;
- Encourage the use of study groups, panel discussions, role-playing, and debates.

How can we make accommodations for **visual learners**? Provide word walls, list reading and content area vocabulary, and post wall charts or hang mobiles from the ceiling sharing skills recently taught to act as valuable reminders for visual students. Keep classroom lights on, as the brain needs light to efficiently perform and learn. Recently, a speaker at the Mid-Hudson Reading Council advised teachers to avoid turning off the lights while using an overhead projector, since lights off encourage the brain to shut down. However, according to Dunn, Dunn, and Price (1989), "fluorescent lighting overstimulates certain learners and causes hyperactiviity and restlessness."

Auditory learners will benefit from being able to use headphones to hear and read along with taped books or lectures. Most auditory learners prefer quiet space to avoid distraction.

Kinesthetic learners profit from moving to learning centers and working with hands-on materials. It is important to have a variety of supplies available. Even college students are more engaged and say that they remember new material better when they have the opportunity to do a hands-on projects. Some "jittery" kids benefit from just being allowed to stand during class. We found it best to seat these children at the back of the room or on side aisles, so they wouldn't block other learners. It worked like a charm!

Cindy Montgomery is quoted in Reading Today as saying, "If they don't learn the way you teach, teach the way they learn." (2005, p. 46). This shows us that, as teachers, we must remain flexible and open.

Environment Matters

Light, temperature, noise, furniture/setting design, and time of day are environmental factors influencing learning, according to researchers. We need to customize the classroom environment as much as possible, to accommodate different learners.

There is a distinct and proven link between illumination and student achievement as indicated in the National Clearinghouse for Education study, "Do School Facilities Affect Academic Outcomes?"

"These reports document

- there are optimal lighting levels for learning,
- appropriate lighting improves test scores and reduces poor behavior,
- daylight fosters higher student achievement."

Ideally, light levels in a classroom should reflect the characteristics of **natural light**, to keep the brain engaged and active. Clearly, correct illumination is a critical component of teaching and learning (McCreery & Hill, 2003). What can we learn from this? As much as possible, increase the amount of natural light in your classroom. Raising and opening blinds, while making it impossible to hang charts and posters, allows for more natural light for the students.

- If it is too hot in the room, many students cannot concentrate; yet if it's too cold, other learners have trouble staying on task. As teachers, however, we rarely have control over the classroom temperature.

- Some students require quiet to learn while others learn best surrounded by sound. This presents some difficulties. We have had students ask for permission to work outside the classroom, to limit distractions caused by classroom noise. There were even some students who preferred to work under the teacher's desk to lower the noise factor.

- We all know students who need to have a desk away from the rest of the class in order to work, while others work best when desks are grouped together. So how do we optimize our classroom for all students? One of our colleagues brought corrugated refrigerator boxes into her class, painted them, and these provided "private offices" for students needing their own space.

- Elementary schools have been aware that most students are sharpest early in the school day, which is why reading is generally the first subject taught. Conversely, on the high school level, teenagers tend to be sleepy early in the morning, and first and second period classes challenge many. Knowing this, why do most school districts have high schoolers begin early, and elementary school students arrive later in the morning?

Implications for Classroom Teachers

- Many of the study techniques you will find in this text appeal to at least two learning modalities.

- Permit students who get distracted or overstimulated by overhead fluorescent lights to wear baseball caps in order to block the brightness. Likewise, allow students who need light to sit where the natural light source is brightest.

- Accommodate student needs by having some clustered desk grouping and some individual seating arrangements.

- Study carrels, even ones made from appliance boxes, help easily distracted students improve concentration. Allowing a student to work outside the classroom or under the teacher's desk are ways to provide quieter space. Wearing unconnected headphones will block extraneous noise.

- Here's a factoid from Don Campbell, musicologist, that may prove useful in your class. The *right* ear is better for more logical information and the *left* ear is more for feelings, emotions, and pleasures. That means the ideal in your teaching is to situate yourself to talk more often on the left side of the room (seen as you face the class) and play music on the right side of the class (Jensen, 1995).

"No two children are alike and no two children learn in the identical way. An enriched environment for one is not necessarily enriched for another."
—Marian Diamond, Professor of Neuroanatomy at Berkeley

"The one who is immersed in the experience is the one who is learning."
—Pat Wolfe

SUMMARY OF KEY CONCEPTS IN THIS CHAPTER

- Discover what factors affect learning.
    - –Visual learners use both pictures and print.
    - –Auditory learners profit from listening and speaking.
    - –Kinesthetic/tactile learners need to touch and move around.
- Utilize Learning Styles Cognitive Preference Inventory.
- Empower V-A-K study strategies.
- Notice Glasser's "We Learn" controversy.
- Understand the importance of environment.
    - –Physical room accommodations aid learners.

3

Rethinking How We Learn

Each Brain is Unique

Is it justifiable to say that one person is more intelligent than another? Can we confidently compare individuals on the basis of intelligence as we compare them, say, on the basis of height or weight?

The answer to both questions is NO! Brain research proposes that we come to knowledge in different ways and that some of us are stronger in particular ways of knowing than in others. Moreover, research maintains that all of us who are normal human beings actually come to knowledge, or process information, in a variety of ways, each of us combining those ways in a unique fashion.

WORKING WITH YOUR STRENGTHS

Teachers need to serve as "strength detectives," especially for students who have difficulties. Teach students ways to use their more highly developed abilities to bypass their weaknesses. Every lesson taught in multiple ways will ensure that all students benefit. Not all students are strong in verbal/linguistic and logical/mathematical thinking, yet these are the basis for the majority of teaching in our school systems. Therefore, within a given week in your classroom, students need to be immersed in learning which involves "many ways of knowing." (That does not mean within each lesson!) This way, you will catalyze interest in all students, regardless of their strengths and weaknesses.

Think, if you will, about special education individual education plans (IEP). Every year, special education children are tested to determine their weaknesses and needs. The IEP then shows what gains need to be made in the coming school year. Instead, we suggest identifying the child's strengths in addition to his weaknesses. Suggest strategies using those strengths to build up weaknesses. This "can-do" approach will promote more growth and increase the child's self-esteem. Teaching students to study from their strengths with a "can-do" attitude will increase learning efficiency. Students discover time flies because they're having learning (Reardon, 2006). And learning is serious fun!

DEFINITIONS OF INTELLIGENCE

People often mistakenly use a person's memory capacity to evaluate his or her intelligence. Intelligence is much more than memory. Some aspects of intelligence are innate but much can be done to foster and expand a person's intelligence. According to Dr. Howard Gardner (1983), we are all born with brains that have all the intelligences within; they just develop in different amounts in each individual.

Think about intelligence for a moment. Now, write your personal definition of intelligence. Intelligence is _____

_____

_____

_____.

There are many ways to define intelligence. Robin Fogarty (1997) pointed out several views of intelligence in *Brain Compatible Classrooms*:

- Spearman's (Barrett, 1992) theory of general intelligence states that intelligence is inherited and unchanging and is measured by one's ability to score sufficiently on the Stanford-Binet intelligence test.
- Feurstein's (1980) theory of modifiability states that intelligence is not a fixed entity but rather a function of experience and that it can be changed with human intervention and life experiences.
- Sternberg's (1997) theory of successful intelligence argues for three types of intelligence: analytical intelligence (compare, evaluate, judge, and assess), creative intelligence (invent, imagine, suppose, and design), and practical intelligence (practice, implements, show, and use).
- Perkins's (1995) theory of learnable intelligence states that there is a neural intelligence that contributes to neural efficiency; an experiential intelligence that stores personal experience in diverse situations; and a reflective intelligence that contributes knowledge, understanding, and attitudes about how to use the mind in intelligent behavior.
- Goleman's (1995a) theory of emotional intelligence delineates five elements of the emotional intelligence, including self-awareness (self-confidence and self-decisiveness), self-regulation (controlling impulsivity and handling emotions), motivation (hope, initiative in goal setting, and zeal), empathy (reading others feelings and caring), and social skill (influence, leadership, and team building). Goleman believed that emotional intelligence may be more important than IQ.

- Costa (1991) outlined a set of dispositions as evidence of intelligence. Included in his list of behaviors are persistence, reflectiveness, flexibility, metacognition, problem posing, accuracy, prior knowledge, enjoyment of thinking, and transference. He looked at intelligence in terms of acquired habits of mind, or states of mind.
- Sousa (2001) noted in *How the Brain Learns* that what constitutes human intelligence is growing increasingly complex. It represents a combination of varied abilities and skills. He went on to state that the work of researchers such as Gardner and Sternberg has changed our concept of intelligence from a singular entity to a multifaceted aptitude that varies even within the same person.

Howard Gardner (1983) defined intelligence as

> the ability to create an effective product or offer a service that is valued in one's culture;

> a set of skills that enables an individual to solve problems encountered in life; and

> the potential for finding or creating solutions for problems, which enables a person to acquire new knowledge.

It's the can-do part that counts.

Do any of these definitions strike a responsive chord? Are any of them close to your definition? Probably the best definition includes bits and pieces from each of the experts. Take a moment to rewrite your personal definition of intelligence. Intelligence is _____

_____

_____

_____

_____.

EACH BRAIN IS UNIQUE

Each brain travels at its own speed down its own developmental roadway; the brain of every learner is unique. According to Fogarty (1997), your brain has been custom made for you, and our rewards come not from having brains but using them. "Our brains are continually making new neural connections" (Connell, 2005, p. 69). It's the connections that allow us to solve problems and figure things out. "The knowledge in our minds consists of neural networks in our brains, so if that knowledge is to grow, the neural networks must physically change" (Zull, 2002, as cited in Connell, 2005, p. 69).

While most normal brains have a similar set of systems for sensing, feeling, and thinking, the set is integrated differently in each brain; thus, teaching that is multifaceted with inherent choices and options for the learner fosters optimal learning (Fogarty, 1997). To educate every child, teachers need to present and rehearse information using a variety of techniques since there are innumerable ways each brain responds to instruction. The greater the variety of instructional strategies, the more likely all learners are to succeed. We suggest that teachers help children discover individual learning strengths plus expand their strategies to go beyond their own learning preferences.

Reardon (2006) explained that good teachers reach 70 percent of students (always the same ones). Great teachers also reach 70 percent of their students—but students change daily. "All students can learn and succeed, but not on the same day in the same way," stated William G. Spady (as cited in Kettle & Kagan, 2005, p. 285).

MULTIPLE INTELLIGENCES

"When we help our students make academic connections using different intelligences, we are also helping one part of their brain to link to other parts. Using multiple intelligences that work together helps to connect and strengthen neural pathways in the brain" (Connell, 2005, p. 75).

Both teachers and students will benefit from awareness of their intelligences. Figure 3.1 helps us understand Gardner's eight intelligences. Recently, Gardner (1998, 1999, as cited in Connell, 2005) identified the existential intelligence as a "half intelligence" because he has not been able to find a physiological location for it in the brain. "Existentialists are those concerned, often at an early age, with the big, piercing questions: Who am I? Why do we die? What is the meaning of life?" (Connell, 2005, p. 68) Existential intelligence may coincide with a spiritual awareness and concern for humanity.

Figure 3.1 Eight Ways of Being Smart

Intelligence	Excels At	Learns Best When	Related Careers
Verbal/ Linguistic	reading, writing, creating, and perceiving rhymes and inflection	reading, writing, telling stories, thinking in words	authors, attorneys, public speakers, politicians
Mathematical/ Logical	problem-solving, abstract thinking, math, logic, pattern identification	categorizing, classifying, seeing relationships	engineers, mathematicians, researchers, astronomers
Visual/Spatial	drawing, creating charts and diagrams, reading maps, mental visualization, puzzle-solving	using the "mind's eye," working with visual elements, such as pictures, colors, graphic organizers	pilots, architects, surgeons, artists
Body/ Kinesthetic	sports, role-playing, crafts	manipulating materials, using hands-on activities and movement	professional athletes, dancers, jugglers, actors
Musical/ Rhythmic	singing, remembering melodies, identifying rhythm, pitch and tonality, keeping the beat, appreciating music	putting ideas to music, using rhythm and rhyme, listening to music	conductors, composers, music critics, performers
Interpersonal	understanding other people, identifying moods and intentions, leading, communicating	working in cooperative groups, sharing, talking to others	teachers, religious leaders, therapists, politicians
Intrapersonal	meta-cognitive thinking, goal setting, self-perception	working alone, reflecting upon and evaluating self-learning	philosophers, psychologists, novelists
Naturalist	classifying patterns, appreciating nature, identifying plants and animals	working in nature, identifying patterns, observing living things	naturalists, botanists, environmental engineers

MULTIPLE INTELLIGENCES INVENTORY

We have included a quick, easy-to-administer multiple intelligences inventory developed to use with all grade levels including graduate students and teachers. Read the list of indicators (see Figure 3.2) describing characteristics within each of the eight intelligence areas. Students indicate under each intelligence (labeled "smarts") which represents the amount of intelligence they feel best describes them, ranging from "tons" to "just a little bit" (see Figure 3.3). Please note that there is no category labeled "none at all," since we each possess, to at least some slight degree, all of the intelligences. Some students color in the entire space, some put a check mark or an "X" in the space, and some draw designs in each one. We've also had some students who fill in the space halfway between two categories, indicating they do not feel that they fit completely in just one area. For example, a mark can be made in the bottom half of "a good deal" and the top half of "some."

Figure 3.2

The Eight Smarts Self-Evaluation Indicators

An asterisk (*) indicates that a statement is more appropriate for older students or adults.

Word Smart

A student with tons of word smarts might say the following:
- I love to read.
- I get excited when my teacher tells the class that we're going to be creating our own stories.
- Although classroom presentations make me a little nervous, I begin to feel comfortable when I begin speaking.
- When I learn a new vocabulary word, I try to use it in my conversation or writing.
- I am good at using words to describe things or persuade others.
- I enjoy word games like Scrabble and crossword puzzles.
- Hanging out in a bookstore or library is a perfect way to spend an afternoon.
- *I speak using metaphors and expressive language.
- *Explaining things or arguing a point energizes me.

Logic Smart

A student with tons of logic smarts might say the following:
- I enjoy solving challenging math problems.
- I prefer math to social studies and English classes.
- I understand charts and diagrams with numbers.
- It's fun to play games that require tactics and strategies.
- I enjoy using a computer.

(continued)

- I often find myself discovering patterns.
- *I take little on faith alone.
- *I am comfortable with abstract ideas.
- *I believe there is a logical explanation for almost everything.

Picture Smart

A student with tons of picture smarts might say the following:
- I get excited when my teacher asks the class to draw or make a creative project about a book we are reading.
- I can easily picture something in my mind and draw it.
- I doodle when I think.
- Drawing diagrams, lines, and arrows helps me understand ideas.
- I like to arrange pictures in photo albums and bulletin boards.
- I remember faces better than names.
- *I am good at matching colors and decorating.
- *I read maps easily.
- *I can stand in one location and visualize things from different locations without moving.

Body Smart

A student with tons of body smarts might say the following:
- I spend time after school playing different types of sports.
- I am full of energy and get "itchy" if I can't move around.
- I enjoy role-playing.
- I am able to learn new sports or dances easily.
- Moving and manipulating things helps me understand how they work.
- Watching sports is less interesting than playing them.
- I talk with my hands.
- I like hands-on activities such as knitting, building models, jewelry making, and shoveling snow.
- *I am good at mimicking other people's physical behavior.

Music Smart

A student with tons of music smarts might say the following:
- I can easily follow the beat of songs and remember songs' words after hearing them a few times.
- I enjoy singing, even to myself.
- I can play a musical instrument well.
- I use familiar jingles to remember information for a test.
- I often hum without even realizing it.
- I am good at keeping a beat.
- I enjoy being in musical performances.
- I frequently listen to music.
- *It drives me crazy when music is off-key, off-time, or flat.

(continued)

People Smart

A student with tons of people smarts might say the following:
- I enjoy being with other students and like the fact that we're all different.
- Parties and making new friends are fun.
- I love to study people in other cultures.
- I would rather be with my friends or family than be alone.
- When my friends have a problem, they come to me for advice.
- I am good at making people feel comfortable and am easy to get to know.
- *Sometimes the best part of a trip is meeting new people.

Self-Smart

A student with tons of self-smarts might say the following:
- I know myself well and often think about my strengths and weaknesses.
- I daydream a lot about things I want to do in the future.
- "Independent" describes me.
- I march to the beat of a different drummer.
- I like to think things through before I take action.
- I like things I can do alone, like computer games, solitaire, and exercise.
- I frequently need alone time.
- *Setting personal goals is important to me.
- *I value my own judgment over what I hear or read.

Nature Smart

A student with tons of nature smarts might say the following:
- Whenever possible, I enjoy being outdoors.
- Surrounding myself with flowers and plants makes me happy.
- I can identify different birds, butterflies, and trees.
- Camping and hiking are my favorite vacations.
- I get involved trying to solve environmental problems.
- I need to play outside after school.
- *I prefer biology to physics.
- *Painting or taking pictures of things in nature is pleasurable.
- *I can tell when it's going to rain by identifying rain clouds.
- *I like spending time gardening.

The inventory goal is to help students and teachers become aware of their strengths and then use them to increase their less-developed intelligences. For example, someone strong in logical intelligence can use logic to attack a weakness in spatial intelligence—by logically thinking through the problem step-by-step to orient spatially and reach the correct solution. A student who is weak in spelling but strong artistically could draw rebus pictures to remember how to spell a troublesome word. This paradigm shift will open the minds of teachers and students to study in new ways—both stronger and smarter.

Figure 3.3 "Eight Smarts" Self-Evaluation

Eight Smarts	Word Smart	Logic Smart	Picture Smart	Body Smart	Music Smart	People Smart	Self Smart	Nature Smart
Tons								
A Good Deal								
Some								
Just a Little Bit								

We have found that students generally use a combination of several intelligences as they work. A football player is an example of this. Before executing a pass, the player uses logic to know where a receiver will be, visual/spatial to determine how hard to throw the ball, and body/kinesthetic intelligence to actually pass the ball. Additionally, all players depend on strong interpersonal skills for successful teamwork.

TEACHER MULTIPLE INTELLIGENCES REFLECTIONS

Completing this inventory will guide teachers in reflecting on how they use their own intelligences in teaching and identify ways to improve instruction.

Figure 3.4 Teacher Multiple Intelligences Reflections

1. My personal intelligence strengths include:

2. The lessons I teach typically include the following intelligences:

3. The intelligences I enjoy most in my students are:

4. Intelligences I usually do not incorporate in my teaching are:

5. Ways I can consciously include the intelligences that I normally do not use in my teaching are:

6. Find a colleague and discuss strategies to help you utilize those overlooked intelligences in your teaching.

We challenge you to intentionally use a minimum of one other way of knowing and learning in each lesson!

(Adapted from Nicholson-Nelson, 1998.)

UNRECOGNIZED BRILLIANCE

Teachers and peers don't always recognize creativity, intelligence, and imagination in children. History is full of examples of people who didn't take, or weren't given, the chance to experience the joy of learning during their school years. Do you know the following?

- Albert Einstein was four years old before he could speak and seven before he could read.
- Beethoven's music teacher once said of him, "As a composer, he is hopeless."
- Leo Tolstoy flunked out of college.
- A newspaper editor fired Walt Disney because he had "no good ideas."
- Abraham Lincoln entered the Black Hawk War as a captain and came out as a private.
- Louisa May Alcott was told by an editor that she would never write anything that had popular appeal.
- Winston Churchill failed the sixth grade.
- Isaac Newton did poorly in grade school.

- Thomas Edison's teachers told him that he was too stupid to learn anything.
- Wernher von Braun flunked ninth-grade algebra.
- Admiral Richard Byrd had been retired from the navy, declared "unfit for service," when he flew over both poles.
- Orville Wright was expelled from sixth grade for bad behavior.
- Ben Franklin only went to school from age eight to ten.
- Robin Williams was voted least likely to succeed in high school.
- Charles Schulz (*Peanuts* cartoonist) failed all subjects in eighth grade and flunked algebra, Latin, English, and physics in high school.
- Jay Leno's fifth grade teacher said, "If Jay spent as much time studying as he does trying to be a comedian, he'd be a big star."

NO AVERAGE CHILD

The following anonymously written poem "The Average Child," found in the *Brain Compatible Classroom* (Fogarty, 1997), makes us profoundly aware of the plight of the "average" child, who has yet to discover his or her strengths. Until we recognize there are many different definitions of intelligence, and therefore, many different approaches to teaching and learning, we will have classrooms peopled with many "average" children. We also run the risk of never igniting that special spark to enable students to be more than average. There is a **special** intelligence in every "average" child.

"The Average Child"

I don't cause teachers trouble
my grades have been okay.
I listen in my classes
and I am in school every day.

My teachers think I am average
my parents think so too.
I wish I didn't know that
cause there is lots I would like to do.

I would like to build a rock
I have a book that tells you how,
Or start a stamp collection
well, no use in trying now.

'Cause since I found I am average
I am just smart enough you see
to know there is nothing special
that I should expect of me.

I am part of that majority
that hump part of the bell
who spends his life unnoticed
in an average kind of hell.

The fact is, the more children feel they have abilities, the more success they will experience. They will discover that they **know more than they thought they knew!**

Howard Gardner (1983) told us "there's nothing in the world that can be taught in only one way."

We have added to that "there's nothing in the world that can be studied and learned in only one way."

"You can never say no to intelligence."

—Fogarty

*"Inquiring minds **want** to know."*

—author unknown

"Each one of us has a gift. There is . . . the tortoise gift of the plodder, the fox gift of cunning, the dog gift of faithfulness, the song-sparrow gift of cheerfulness, the swan gift of beauty in motion."

—Hughes Mearnes

SUMMARY OF KEY CONCEPTS IN THIS CHAPTER

- Working with each child's strengths; foster a "can-do" approach.
- Visit various definitions of intelligence and rewrite your own.
- Each brain is unique.
- There are multiple intelligences (see multiple intelligences inventory and teacher reflection).
- There is unrecognized brilliance.
- There is no average child.

CURRICULUM MATERIALS
BALDWIN WALLACE UNIVERSITY

4

This Way to a Healthy Brain

The All-Important *"TIONS"*

The brain is involved in everything we do and everything we are. Dr. Daniel Amen (2005) said, "I learned that when your brain works right, you work right, and that when your brain is troubled, you have trouble in life. Brain health is essential to all aspects of the quality of life" (p. xi). **To be your best self, you must have a brain that works at its best.** Why, then, do we not teach our students to care for and love their brains? Amen (2006) said at the Learning Brain Expo, "Most people have no love for their brains—they care more about their faces, bellies, and butts!" A healthy brain needs a strong, healthy physical body to perform at its best. Karen Cohen (n.d.) has suggested that the brain is strongly influenced (both positively and negatively) by our physical condition.

THE *"TIONS"* OF A HEALTHY BRAIN

Good schools can raise IQ scores and poor schools can lower them according to Eric Jensen (2006). Tapping into the power and energy of the body is necessary for superior mental and emotional performance. Key factors that aid academic success are the following **"tions"**: nutri**tion**, hydra**tion**, oxygena**tion**/activa**tion** (exercise), motiva**tion**, emo**tion**, protec**tion**, affirma**tion**, and the body's needed restora**tion** gained through sleep. Making students aware of the critical **"tions"** will enable them to maximize their brains' potential. Even with a diverse knowledge of study skills, students will not reach their potential without the body and brain tuning achieved when the **"tions"** become part of their lives.

THE PHYSICAL "TIONS"

Nutrition

If you want your marks to race along the super highway to success, your body needs premium fuel (super nutrition) from brain-empowering foods. The brain, which is only 2 percent of our body mass, consumes nearly 20 percent of our calories. (Moretz, 2006). "Good nutrition, combined with great study habits, can make your report card something to be proud of." (Growing Alberta , 2005).

Critical to every child's success is a great brain breakfast every day. "Glucose is a major nutrient used by the brain and glucose is most depleted after a night's sleep." (Office of Teaching Effectiveness and Faculty Development, 2001, paragraph 4). Children get about one-fourth of their nutrient needs from breakfast. If they skip breakfast, their performance in school will be impaired. The Connecticut Parent Teacher Association (n.d.) stated that the effects of not having breakfast are (a) decreased attention span and ability to concentrate, (b) restlessness, (c) less energy and enthusiasm, and (d) poor academic achievement. That's a big price to pay for eliminating a meal—so don't leave home without it! The Scholastic Web site, in "Back to School: Start Smart" (n.d.), stated, "Breakfast is the food of champions—not just athletic stars, but academic ones too." The article goes on to cite the Children's Nutrition Research Center at Baylor College of Medicine's statement that "eating breakfast can improve your child's memory, grades, school attendance, and punctuality." Oatmeal is considered one of the best choices for breakfast because it delivers a good mix of carbohydrates, fiber, and protein. It may also boost your child's memory! The converse is also true—avoid high-sugar cereals and high-fat foods.

Several sources have suggested the following list of foods as being nutritionally beneficial for our brains. (Amen, 2006; Pratt & Matthews, 2004; Sprenger, 2006)

avocado	oranges
beans	pumpkin (and pumpkin seeds)
blueberries (brainberries) and other berries	red peppers
	salmon (wild preferred)
broccoli	soy
chocolate (only dark!)	spinach
dairy (low-fat)	tea (green and black)
oats	tomatoes (cooked or raw)
olive oil	turkey
olives	yogurt (non-fat)

What can you do to encourage students to add them to their diet?

_____

_____

_____

A nutritious lunch is equally important, since one-third of a child's daily calories are eaten at lunch. Glucose is the fuel that keeps the brain working, and researchers have found that learning tasks quickly deplete the brain's glucose store; a good lunch is required to replenish it. The best brain-boosting glucose sources for lunch include whole fruit (high-fiber choices), canned fruit (water packed), raw vegetables, grilled or steamed vegetables, legumes, and whole- grain products. These are all complex carbohydrates, as opposed to high-sugar foods, such as cookies and candy, which will impair rather than enhance brain function. And, as we all know, sugar has lots of empty calories with no nutritional value, and most of us are allergic to sugar—we "break out in fat!"

Implications for Classroom Teachers

- Teach children the importance of good nutrition and how it helps them study and learn. Repeat frequently.
- Keep a supply of nutritious foods in your classroom for any child who comes to school without having breakfast. Those children need a brain boost.
- Provide a time for children to have a snack—but insist that it be a healthy snack, limited to items on a list of acceptable foods.
- Send a newsletter home, and/or post nutritional information on your class Web site.
- Avoid providing rewards in the form of sugary, high-calorie treats.
- Check out an excellent Web site: www.nutrition.gov.

Hydration

Did you know that brain tissue is 85 percent water? Therefore, the brain is quite sensitive to dehydration. As Karen Cohen (n.d.) teaches us, "Ample hydration allows the brain to function most efficiently, much like grease on gears. Conversely, dehydration slows the brain and is a major factor in fatigue." Cohen also went on to state, "For maximum benefit drink 48–64 ounces of water per day. The benefits extend far beyond boosting your brainpower to support the health of your entire being."

Implications for Classroom Teachers

- Allow students to keep a water bottle with them at their desks.
- Model by drinking water during class.
- Allow students to go to the class drinking fountain when needed.
- Give students a water break at appropriate times, such as after recess or gym.
- Teach students the relationship between hydration and brain health.

Oxygenation/Activation (Exercise)

"Exercise nourishes the brain with oxygen while cleansing the body of performance damaging chemicals. Exercise relieves the body of stress and its by-products to create clearer, more creative thinking. It is well established that we learn and perform better when we feel good. Exercise is a major key to peak performance that powerfully supports academic and personal success." (Cohen, n.d.). The California Department of Health has found that "children who are physically fit are more likely to have higher test scores. The reasons why lead us back to their brains. The part of the brain that processes movement is the same part that processes learning, specifically memory, language, attention, spatial perception, and nonverbal cues."

Teach children deep breathing (diaphragmatic breathing) to help oxygenate their brains. Straightening and lowering the diaphragm and contracting these muscles increases lung capacity.

1. Direct students to sit tall and straight at their desks, with their feet flat on the floor. Ask them to place a hand just below their waists, with their thumbs on their belly buttons, to feel the diaphragm expand.

2. Inhale through the nose to the count of four to deeply fill the lungs with air.

3. Hold, to the count of two to four,—whatever is comfortable.

4. Exhale through the nose or the mouth as if blowing out a candle very slowly to the count of eight.

5. Repeat this simple breathing exercise, working up to ten repetitions.

Since the brain uses one fifth of the body's oxygen, these oxygenation breaks are important. Additionally, they relax the body and calm the mind.

Implications for Classroom Teachers

- Give students a quick stand-and-stretch break every fifteen to thirty minutes. Tie it in with a stand-and-share content review.
- Suggest that students stand, push their chairs under the desks, and lean over the chairs to work at their desks. (Chapman, 2005).
- Intersperse body/kinesthetic study activities into your instruction. See Chapter 6.
- Let students generate and lead oxygenator exercises. (See *Brain Gym* by Paul and Gail Dennison [1986] for additional ideas; www.braingym.com.)
- Lead children in the following exercise, which improves circulation and posture, tones the muscles, and increases oxygen intake.

Swing Those Arms

Directions:

1. Stand with your feet shoulder-width apart.

2. Imagine that your lower body is heavy, your upper body is light, and your head is suspended by an imaginary wire. Let your head and neck relax.

3. Look to a point just slightly higher than straight ahead.

4. To start, let your arms hang at your sides with palms facing up and fingers straight.

5. Raise your arms forward to a horizontal position without bending the elbows, and then let them swing backward under their own power.

6. Repeat. Make the movements continuous; —that is, don't pause at any point either forward or backward. Imagine that your arms are pendulums in a grandfather clock.

7. A rhythm of fifty-five swings per minute—about one "tick" per second—provides the maximum benefit. As you swing, keep your arms comfortably straight without locking your elbows. Be sure to keep your fingers straight, too. Continue the swinging for about five minutes.

8. You may feel tingling in your hands and fingers, which is a sign of increased circulation. You may also feel warmth in your chest and face as well.

9. Once you've stopped all movements, gently shift your weight from side to side before picking up your feet. This will help you avoid dizziness when you take your first steps after finishing.

10. Doing this exercise before a test will likely increase test performance. To maximize learning, students can also be encouraged to use this exercise at home before studying.

Thanks to Carol Martoccia, SIFU, and Master Phil Sant

Fifteen minutes before a test, encourage students to:

- drink 8 ounces of water;
- eat a piece of fruit; and
- do a cross-lateral exercise (Redenbach, 2002).

Cross-Laterals

Cross-laterals are brain "wake-ups." They force the left and right brain hemispheres to talk to each other. Try touching the left elbow to the right knee, then the right elbow to the left knee. Repeat ten times.

Another brain wake-up is to cross your arms across your chest. Pay attention to which hand is on top. Now, reverse the top arm to the bottom. This will feel awkward which brings the brain to instant attention! A variation is to fold your hands together. Note which thumb is on top, and reverse the way the hands are folded. It, too, will feel strange.

"Restoration"—Sleep

When faced with a problem, many people say, "Let me sleep on it." There's probably more wisdom in this old adage than people realize, as the brain clears extraneous debris from the memory during sleep, as stated by Markowitz and Jensen (1999). From Wilson and McNaughton (1994) we discovered that "Our brain completely shuts out new external input during sleep time and instead processes information previously obtained" (pp. 676–679). The combination of processing new information while removing unneeded data enables us to subconsciously solve many problems.

One of the major problems in our society is sleep deprivation (Sprenger, 2002), which decreases brain function. "People who get less than seven hours of sleep a night have lower activity in the temporal lobes, the part of the brain involved in learning and memory" (Amen, 2005, p. 86). Lacking sleep restoration hampers the ability to learn and remember, and impairs concentration, judgment, reaction time, and the ability to retain difficult memory tasks (Markowitz, 1999; Sprenger, 2002). "Sleep-deprived students score poorer on memory and math tests, have lower grades in school, and are at much greater risk for driving accidents" (Amen, 2005, p. 87). Young children need ten hours of sleep, and adults need eight. Teens have been found to need more than nine hours in order to function well and remain alert during the day, possibly because the hormones critical to growth and sexual maturation are released mostly during sleep (Wolfe, 2003). The last two to three hours of sleep is when the brain practices and rehearses new learning. This "instant replay" consolidates and enhances memory, which is why our last few hours of sleep are so valuable (Jensen, 1998). Given that sleep is a time when brain cells replenish themselves and where connections made during the day are strengthened, sleep deprivation can have a major negative effect on learning and memory (Wolfe, 2003).

Any teacher working in a middle school or high school recognizes the difficulty first-period students have paying attention in class. They are quiet and difficult to engage in discussion. Some even fall asleep! "Teachers of early morning classes complain that their students seem to be in class in body only, frequently nodding off, or at the least, drowsy and difficult to teach. Teens' biological clocks appear to be set later than those of children or adults. Most teenage brains aren't ready to wake up until 8 or 9 in the morning, well past the time when the first bell has sounded at most high schools" (Wolfe, 2003). Based on test results, early morning students don't seem to learn as much as students tested later in the day do.

Implications for Classroom Teachers

- Make students aware of this information. Periodically, give them a homework assignment, to "get at least 9 hours of sleep"—especially before a big test!
- Communicate the importance of sleep to parents, via the class newsletter or Web site.
- Encourage parents to support their children in not overprogramming their schedules, thereby enabling them to get sufficient sleep.
- Lobby for opening high schools and middle schools later in the morning and have elementary schools open first.

THE FEELING "TIONS"

Motivation

You can lead a horse to water, but you can't make him drink.

Likewise, you can send a child to school, but you can't make him think.

People are motivated in different ways. Teachers affect the classroom environment through their expectations and the ways these expectations are both communicated and modeled. When teachers model the joys of learning, it can't help but seep into the students.

Goals provide a strong motivation for doing what is needed. There are two parts to goal setting: desired objectives and how to achieve them. Students are either intrinsically motivated to achieve—their drive to attain the objective comes from within—or extrinsically motivated, using either rewards or punishments. The ultimate goal is to have students so turned on and excited that they develop the intrinsic desire to learn. External rewards, such as toys, stickers, candy, and money for grades, all tend to reduce intrinsic motivation and provide only short-term value, since these rewards give the message that learning is not the goal—prizes are.

Some excellent alternatives to rewards that encourages the love of learning for its own sake are:

- providing choices
- encouraging constructivist classes where student interests are paramount
- teaching to preferred learning modalities
- providing hands-on experiences
- including novelty
- giving positive feedback

Implications for Classroom Teachers

- Begin with simple tasks to encourage success. Then gradually increase difficulty level.
- Model and encourage students to celebrate successes.

- Remember—nothing breeds success like success!
- Guide students to set quarterly goals and list behaviors needed to reach those goals. Share with others to get support. Work to achieve the goals and keep promises to themselves.
- Provide consistent feedback and positive support to unmotivated students working toward new behavior patterns.
- In a one-to-one conversation, discuss the fears or difficulties that cause students to feel stuck. Brainstorm new strategies.
- Develop internal motivation with games, relays, drama, and music that empower students.

Protection

Illustration by Bruce Wasserman

Often subtle and difficult for teachers to detect, these emotional threats hinder students from working to their full potential. There is no quick and easy fix to rid a classroom of these threats;, however, one effective way to promote a safe environment for all is to begin the school year teaching Gail Dusa's (1992) life rules.

UPR

1. **Unconditional Positive Regard**. Commonly known as **UPR**, Unconditional Positive Regard defines how to be respectful. Clarify by explaining:

    Regard means to think about how we look at anything.

    Positive means to look on the good side of things.

    Unconditional means without judgment.

    Thus, we define UPR as *to think or look on the positive (good) aspects, without judgment.*

Illustration by Bruce Wasserman

2. **No Put-Downs**. We've all heard the saying, "Sticks and stones will break my bones, but names will never harm me." Well, that's not true. Words can harm us. The teacher must model what is meant by "put-downs," as people (teachers as well as students) use them without realizing that they could be hurting others. Examples might include: "How could you be so dumb?", "You jerk!", "Duh!", and "Shut- up!" or self put-downs, such as: "I can't believe I was so stupid!" All put-downs must be avoided. Did you know it takes five praises to undo just one put-down? That knowledge is a powerful motivator; it makes students stop and think hard! Likewise, sarcasm has no place in any classroom, at any grade level, by either the students or the teacher. Saying "just kidding" does not excuse the use of sarcasm, put-downs, teasing, or harsh words. Unless hurtful verbal comments are eliminated from classrooms, they will not be safe places for children.

T. T. T.

3. **Tell the Truth.** Lead a discussion on the consequences of lying and explain how if you always tell the truth, you never have to remember what you said.

Dare to Dream

4. **Dare to Dream**. As we put dreams into words, verbalization is the first step in making them a reality. It opens the door for positive feedback and support from others. If you can dream it, it will be! Create an atmosphere of respect so students will comfortably dream and grow.

After you have taught these "life rules" the first week of school, use them as a springboard for cooperatively writing specific classroom behaviors. Frequently refer to them throughout the year. Building a safe environment creates the atmosphere of protection so all students can thrive.

Walk your talk
Say what you mean—and mean what you say !

We know that the emotions we feel about individual students, a class as a whole, or a subject —will be communicated via voice and body language—whether we plan to say it or not. **"Our words, our actions, our facial expressions, and our body language must all be congruent"** (Sprenger, 2002, p. 40). Both Sprenger (2002) and Severson (2006) tell us that messages we deliver are *7 percent content*, *38 percent voice* (tonality, tempo, timbre, and volume) and *55 percent body language* (position, proximity, and gestures).

Affirmation—Feedback

The brain is designed to survive and thrive by learning and getting feedback, the process of giving information to a person to help improve performance. Both positive and negative feedback are needed, providing the reinforcement students need to remain motivated (Sprenger, 2005). The best feedback is genuine, specific, immediate, and sometimes dramatic, and is presented in an appropriate form, looking for what can be improved. Positive feedback is effective when conducted in the presence of others, but constructive criticism needs to be done privately. Feedback that encourages dialogue and is reflective, inviting pupils to comment, will leave both parties feeling positive. Praise is most effective when directed toward a task—not toward a person—and when it pinpoints the positive attributes of a student's work or behavior. Whether written or spoken, phrasing feedback using "I" messages shows *how* the speaker feels and *why*. It enables the recipient to internalize positively: "Wow—I achieved my goal!," It is time consuming to be specific, but it pays off in increased student self-esteem and confidence.

- "I can see your studying strategies helped you ace this test."
- "I like how you worded that paragraph. It gives a clear picture of what you were thinking."
- "I am pleased all your digits were lined up perfectly. That made all your answers correct."
- "I am impressed with how you exercised self-control when you didn't respond to . . ."

Immediate feedback helps maintain student attention and interest. It can be a Post-it note placed on the corner of a student's desk, acknowledging something well done, with a thumbs-up. It can be a hand on the shoulder, with a verbal "I" message, sharing your appreciation.

Feedback does not have to be teacher initiated—it can be initiated by fellow classmates: through peer editing; group evaluations, presentations, and projects; pair share; checklists; and rubrics. (Jensen, 1998). Students enjoy giving and receiving feedback when it is presented in the format of "two stars and a wish." The two stars are two positive comments on work shared, and the wish is for clarification, elaboration, or more information.

Emotions

Emotions color almost every brain function. All learning, every memory created, is tagged with emotional markers (Moretz, 2006). Strong emotions can either impede or positively affect how we receive information. "The brain is biologically programmed to attend first to information that has strong emotional content" (Wolfe, 2001, p. 87). An optimal level of emotion is necessary for learning to occur. Like the *Goldilocks Principle*, too much or too little emotion reduces learning efficiency. An optimal level of emotion is "just right" and necessary for learning to occur.

The teachers with great passion are the ones that we remember; our emotions were stirred! Unfortunately, the converse is also true. Boring, uninspiring teachers produce disinterested students, and little, if any, learning. Emotions have the power to be either a roadblock or a smooth ride to long-term memory, and they are key to effective teaching and studying. "Emotion is the strongest force in the brain" (Tileston, 2004, p. 73).

Implications for Classroom Teachers

Throughout this book, ways to add emotion to your teaching will be identified with an "e"-hook.

e

- Since emotions are contagious, it is important to show enthusiasm and make presentations exciting.
- The brain loves to learn through stories that personalize information.
- Identifying oneself with characters creates strong connections. This is why historical fiction, biographies, and books like *The Magic School Bus* series stimulate interest.
- Creating wild, bizarre stories about any content being studied will also personalize and embed the information in long-term memory.
- Encourage students to remember events in their lives that relate to new concepts.
- Using humor triggers attention and aids retention.
- Music, simulations, and role-play create strong emotional pathways.
- Real-life problem solving motivates.
- Activities such as role-plays, simulations, debates, and discussions all provide emotional hooks to facilitate recall.
- "AHA" moments for students signal strong emotional connections.
- Celebrate learning successes.

"Emotion drives attention, and attention drives learning."

—Robert Sylwester

"We learn with our minds, hearts, and bodies."

—Eric Jensen

"How your brain works determines how happy you are, how effective you feel, and how well you interact with others."

—Dr. Daniel Amens

"Emotion is often a more powerful determinant of our behavior than our brains' logical rational processes."

—Robert Sylwester

Strong emotions = strong memory links
Watch for "e"-hook alerts throughout the book signifying an activity with strong emotional hooks to the brain.

SUMMARY OF KEY CONCEPTS IN THIS CHAPTER

- Essential brain health. When all the "tions" are attended to, the brain is ready to address study skills!
- The All-Important **"tions"**
    The Physical **"tions"**
    - Nutrition and Teaching Implications
    - Hydration and Teaching Implications
    - Oxygenation/Activation (Exercise) and Teaching Implications
    - "Restoration"—Sleep and Teaching Implications
    The Feeling **"tions"**
    - Motivation and Teaching Implications
    - Protection
      –Life rules
        –Unconditional Positive Regard
        –No Put-Downs
        –Tell the Truth
        –Dare to Dream
      –Say what you mean and mean what you say
    - Affirmation—Feedback
    - Emotions and Teaching Implications
        –"e"-hooks mark strategies with strong emotional connectors

5

Be-Boppin' the Brain

Musical Rhythmic Studying

Be-boppin' the brain **raises IQ.**
It makes connections the whole body through.

Columbus sailed the ocean blue.
We learned this **quickly**, that is true.

Learning it was quite a breeze,
And we can **retrieve** it with lots of ease.

When we use music, we **exercise** our **brain**.
No longer does our body feel a drain.

Verbal memory grows quite well.
We don't forget words, so we feel swell.

Higher forms of **thinking** no longer are a strain,
As we use music to activate the brain.

Spatial intelligence and **mathematics** gain.
Music makes them grow—that's very plain.

When music is used, remembering's no deal.
We **learn** facts **fast**—and smart we feel!

Here's what we've learned from experts:
- Lazear (2004) wrote that the "musical-rhythmic intelligence probably has a stronger consciousness-altering effect than do any of the other intelligences. We use music, rhythm, sound or vibrations to instantly shift our mood or awareness" (p. 55).
- Brain research shows that music is not only fun, but also improves our brain development and even enhances skills in other subjects such as reading and math (Weinberger, 1998).

- Researchers tell us students easily recall the words and music to all their favorite songs. We need to take advantage of the brain's ability to remember information set to music. Think about the many songs you can recite.
- Scientists believe music trains the brain for higher forms of thinking.
- Music engages the whole body, as well as the brain. A recent study done by neurologist Frank Wilson showed that when a musician plays music, he uses 90 percent of his brain. Wilson could find no other activity that uses the brain to this extent. Therefore, he concluded that a child who is playing a musical instrument or singing on a regular basis is exercising the entire brain (Wilson, as cited in Silberg, 1998). No wonder it is so much easier to remember information that is sung!
- "Study after study has demonstrated that the process of learning to read and play music actually stimulates important areas of the brain. This can lead to accelerated rates of learning and comprehension in math, science and reading which, in turn, results in improved attitudes toward learning and better behavior in school" (Chan, 2003, p. 3).
- In a news article entitled: "Mozart Effect or Not, Music is Good for the Brain," a Canadian study lends support to the idea that musical training may do more for kids than simply teach them their scales—it exercises parts of the brain useful in mathematics, spatial intelligence, and other intellectual pursuits (Poughkeepsie Journal, July 18, 2004).
- Music has the ability to facilitate language acquisition, reading readiness, and general intellectual development; to foster positive attitudes and to lower truancy in middle and high school; to enhance creativity; and to promote social development, personality adjustment, and self-worth (Hanshumaker, 1980, as cited in Weinberger).
- When writing about step-by-step math processes, Kay Smitherman said, "With music, the steps are already implanted in your brain. Students can hum while a test is being taken—it's right there in their heads" (Instructor, 2005).
- When we use music (or melody), we process through the right hemisphere of the brain. Content presented verbally is processed in the left hemisphere. So teaching students to study through the use of music, specifically singing and rapping, enables them to study with their whole brain.
- Anything taught with music, rhythm, or rhyme carries a strong emotional hook into long-term memory.

The well-known tunes that melodiously carry content concepts are called "piggyback songs" (Wolfe, 2001). Students will never forget them—just as each of us can still sing the alphabet song! And how many years ago did we learn that?

Factoid: The tune of the alphabet song is taken from Mozart's "Variations on a Theme" and involves encoding, maintenance plus retrieval, all wrapped up in a neat little package (Redenbach, 2002). Let children bring favorite CDs or MP3 recordings to school. It will give you insight into their favorite music and provide a reservoir of tunes for "piggybacking" information.

Before beginning a short unit on Christopher Columbus, a teacher wanted to activate background knowledge. She asked the class, "What do you already know about Columbus?"

A slew of hands flew up. One or two children shared interesting ideas; then another student proudly announced, "Columbus sailed in 1492."

The teacher responded, "Wow! How'd you remember that?"

"Oh," said the student, "Last year we learned a song. 'In 1492, Columbus sailed the ocean blue.'" The rest of the class nodded in agreement.

What was learned through music stayed with these children.

Figure 5.1 Piggyback picture

Illustration by Bruce Wasserman

Teaching Piggyback Songs

Meish Goldish (2006) suggested, "Before you introduce a mnemonic song to the class, help students think about how music can be a valuable learning tool. Invite volunteers to name or sing songs they've committed to memory in order to recall information. You might explain that the class will be learning mnemonic songs, with lyrics written specifically to bolster what students are learning in the classroom" (p. 6).

Here are some suggestions for teaching these piggyback songs:

- Provide a copy of the piggybacked song or printed lyrics to each student.
- Clap the rhythm of the song. Invite the students to clap the rhythm with you.
- Read the song lyrics in unison. Discuss how the song lyrics connect to the topic being studied and how it will help them remember.
- Sing the first verse of the song and the chorus for the class. Invite students to hum along.
- Ask the class to sing the melody, using "la, la, la" instead of the actual words.
- Now, put it all together. Sing the lyrics, using the piggybacked melody just practiced.
- The following Web sites provide lyrics and audio clips of children's music: www.niehs.nih.gov/kids/music.htm and www.kididdles.com.

Keeping brain research in mind, here are a number of practical ways to study, using musical-rhythmic activities. It is our intent they will be the spark igniting you and your students to develop your own songs, raps, rhymes and cheers as you need them. The following activities are grouped according to content areas: language arts, science, social studies, math, and general knowledge. Have fun traveling the musical-rhythmic road to long-term memory!

Study Strategies In Music

Subject Area: Language Arts

*The Essay Boogie (to the tune of the "Electric Slide")
Written by teachers in the Arlington School District

IT'S AN ESSAY

Use a **topic sentence**	Called a **thesis**	Boogie Woogie Woogie
Explain the **main idea**	It's important	BWW
Now it's time for the **body**	**Three paragraphs**	BWW
Each with a **topic sentence**	**Supporting details**	BWW
At least **five-six sentences**	Don't be stingy	BWW
Have an **ending sentence**	Don't leave us hangin'	BWW
Use sentence **variety**	Mix it up	BWW
Use **first**, **next**, and **after**	No "I", "I", "I"	BWW
No **choppy** sentences	Keep it flowin'	BWW
Wrap up your essay	A **conclusion**	BWW
Restate the main idea	Almost finished	BWW
Edit your essay	It's a **process**	BWW
Grammar and **verb tense**	**Punctuation**	BWW
Indent and **spelling**	**Capitalization**	BWW
So now you know how to	Write an **essay**	BWW
Here, now, and everywhere . . .		

*BINGO Facts (Vowels, colors, and states—or any facts you can fit to the tune of "BINGO")
From If the Shoe Fits . . . by Caroline Chapman

> There was a teacher who had a class
> > And they could say their vowels,
> A-E-I-O-U, A-E-I-O-U, A-E-I-O-U
> > And they could say their vowels.
> There was a teacher who had a class
> > And they could spell their colors,
> P-U-R-P-L-E, P-U-R-P-L-E, P-U-R-P-L-E
> > And they could spell their colors.
> (Note: All color words will fit.)
>
> The U.S.A. has many states
> > And we can learn to spell them.
> G-E-O-R-G-I-A, G-E-O-R-G-I-A, G-E-O-R-G-I-A
> > And we can learn to spell them.
> (Note: All the state names will fit.)

*The Period Song (to the tune of "Row, Row, Row your Boat")
Written by Melinda Borgaard

> Stop, stop, stop the words
> > with a little dot.
> Use a period at the end,
> > so they'll know to stop.

*Parts of Speech
Have your students learn the forty-eight prepositions, twenty-three helping verbs, and eighteen linking verbs by creating their own songs for them and using old, familiar melodies.

*Learn Spelling Words With Songs:

- Any six-letter word can be sung to the tune of: "Happy Birthday."
  Example: *family*
- You can learn to spell seven-letter words to the tune of: "Twinkle, Twinkle Little Star." Repeat the spelling word six times.
  Example: *musical*
- Eight-letter words can be learned by singing "For He's A Jolly Good Fellow."
  Example: *teaching*

The next five songs and raps come from a wonderful book, *Rappin' and Rhymin'*, by Doctor Rosella Wallace, 1992. Used with permission of Zephyr Press, Chicago.

*Parts of Speech Song (to the tune of "When the Saints Go Marching In")

What is a noun?
What is a noun?
We can tell you about a noun.
A noun is the name of:
A person, place, or thing.
What is a verb?
What is a verb?
We can tell you about a verb.
A verb tells what the noun does,
Like: *run* and *saw* and *sing*.

What is an adjective?
What is an adjective?
It is a describing word.
Like *blue* in blue sweater,
And *pretty* in pretty bird.

*The Contraction Song (to the tune of "Oh My Darling Clementine")

I've an apostrophe;
I'm a contraction.
Contraction is my name.
I make two words into one word,
But the meaning stays the same.

Don't change the first word;
Spell it correctly.
It's the second word you'll see
That some letters will be missing,
And a new word I will be.

Put an apostrophe
In the space
Where the letters were left out.
The new word will be shorter—
That's what contractions are all about.

*TH Words Spelling Rap

There's a "HERE" in THERE,
There's a "HEM" in THEM,
There's a "HOSE" in THOSE,
There's a "HAT" in THAT,
What's in THERE, THEM, THOSE, and THAT?

There, them, those, that,
There, them, those, that
Are words we can rap.
THAT'S A FACT!

*City–Comma–State Punctuation Rap

Zero, two, four, six, and eight,
This is the way we punctuate:

City	Comma	State	
City	Comma	State	
City	Comma	City	Comma
City	Comma	State.	

*Question Words Spelling Rap

There's a "HO" in WHO.
W-H-O spells WHO.   *WHO?*

There's a "HAT" in WHAT.
W-H-A-T spells WHAT.   *WHAT?*

There's a "HEN" in WHEN.
W-H-E-N spells WHEN.   *WHEN?*

There's a "HERE" in WHERE.
W-H-E-R-E spells WHERE.   *WHERE?*

There's a "HO" in WHO,
There's a "HAT" in WHAT,
There's a "HEN" in WHEN,
There's a "HERE" in WHERE.

Who, what, when, and where,
Are question words
We spell with a flair.

*Cheer
Carolyn Chapman

Synonyms, synonyms: that's our game
These are words that *mean the same.*
Homonyms, homonyms, that's our game
These are words that *sound the same.*
Antonyms, antonyms, take a hike
These are words that *aren't alike.*

We like to highlight the key words *mean the same, sound the same,* and *aren't alike* with colorful highlighting tape.

*The Well–Known Spelling Rule (around for ages)

I before *E*
Except after *C*
Or when sounded like *A*
As in *neighbor* or *weigh*.

Subject Area: Science

*Cerebellum Song (to the tune of Sarasponda)
Marny Sorgen

Cerebellum, cerebellum, cerebellum
      what's your job?
Cerebellum, cerebellum, cerebellum
      what's your job?
I help you move; coordinated moves,
I tell your muscles what to do and
      help rote memory too.

*Decomposition Rap
    adapted from a choral reading by Steve Van Zandt
    copy from Project WILD, New York State Deparptment of Environmental
    Conservation

The Chorus:
Group 1 says: DE-COMP-osition, DE-COMP-osition (4 times)
   (and rolls arms around and around)
Group 2 says: GET DOWN, BREAK DOWN (4 times)
   (and shakes hands high on "Get Down" and low on "Break Down")

The Rapper:
Is there waste? Well, I don't know
One thing dies, to **let another grow**,
The circle goes round each and every day
It's nature's rap and it's called **decay**.

So come on people gather round, and make the decomposition sound

(CHORUS)

Now there are many kinds of bugs
From **worms** to **snails**, to banana **slugs**,
But, hey, they're useful, that ain't no jive
They help to **keep the soil alive**.

So come on people, no time to nap; we've got to do decomposition rap

(CHORUS)

Decomposition rap is a useful game
Trees **drop their leaves** like the falling rain
Bugs **chew them up**, then **spit them out**,
Making the soil for a new tree to sprout.

So come on people ain't no imposition, the name of the rap is decomposition!

(CHORUS)

Environmental Education students at Purchase College (SUNY) enjoyed this two-part rap.

*Recycle Songs (to the tune of "Twinkle, Twinkle, Little Star"
Written by Jodi Vines, graduate student, SUNY New Paltz

We recycle what we use
Separate things and you should too!
Glass and paper, plastic, tin,
Go in your recycling bin!
We must start now; we can't wait,
Quick, or it will be too late!

(to the tune of "Eensy Weensy Spider)
Written by Jodi Vines, graduate student, SUNY New Paltz

Reduce, reuse, recycle—words that we all know.
We have to save our planet so we can live and grow.
We might be only children but we will try, you'll see
And we can save our planet—it starts with you and me!!

*Rock Rap
Written by Amy Schwed and Janice Melichar-Utter

Sedimentary, sedimentary, hear our chants
Pebbles and skeletons, shells and plants,
Water moving over them was the norm.
Years of pressure into limestone form.

Igneous, igneous, that's my name
Fire formed rocks, my claim to fame
Magma, magma below the earth
Cools and solidifies to gives rocks birth.

Metamorphic, metamorphic, hardest of the three
Heat and pressure caused the changes you see.
Hard rocks forming at a very slow rate,
Quartz to granite and shale to slate.

*Butterfly Cycle (to the tune of "Row, Row, Row Your Boat")
Written by Kathleen Collins, graduate student, SUNY New Paltz

> Hatch, hatch, hatch little egg,
>> I'm so very small.
> Teeny tiny caterpillar,
>> You can't see at all.
>
> Crawl, crawl caterpillar
>> Munching on a leaf.
> Crawling, munching, crawling, munching,
>> Eat and eat and eat.
>
> Form, form chrysalis,
>> I'm a different shape;
> Hanging by a silken thread
>> Until I can escape.
>
> Rest, rest chrysalis,
>> While I change inside.
> Now at last my time has come
>> To be a butterfly.
>
> Stretch, stretch pretty wings,
>> It's a special day:
> Soon they will be strong enough
>> For me to fly away.
>
> Fly, fly butterfly,
>> Fly from flower to tree.
> Find a place to lay my eggs
>> So they can grow like me.

Adding meaningful actions to each stanza will keep more children engaged, and it's fun.

Subject Area: Social Studies

*The Thirteen Colonies (to the tune of "The Brady Bunch")
Written by graduate students at the State University of New York at New Paltz)

> One day when we decided to be independent
> And we knew that it was much more than a hunch
> That these colonies would someday form a country
> We were thirteen and that started our bunch
>
> REFRAIN: Thirteen colonies, thirteen colonies, that's the way we became
>> the United States.

New England has New Hampshire and Massachusetts,
Connecticut and Rhode Island too.
Mid-Atlantic follows with New York,
Pennsylvania, New Jersey, and Delaware.

REFRAIN: Thirteen colonies, thirteen colonies, that's the way we became
the United States.

Below the Mason Dixon it's the South,
with Maryland and the first colony Virginia.
Then comes the Carolinas,
North and South,
And Georgia becomes the last one.

REFRAIN: Thirteen colonies, thirteen colonies, that's the way we became
the United States.

*Twinkle, Twinkle, Where We Are: A Song About the Continents (to the tune of "Twinkle, Twinkle, Little Star")
Written by graduate students at the State University of New York at New Paltz

There are seven continents to know.
We'll learn them all, c'mon let's go.
North America we all know,
South America's down below,
Over the ocean, across the sea,
Europe is the place you'd be,
Asia is the one next door,
Africa's where the lions roar,
Australia, see a kangaroo,
Antarctica, your lips turn blue.

*Factors Affecting Climate (a cadence, with hand movements)
Written by Janice Melichar-Utter

	movements—if desired
LAT-I-TUDE	(hands flat, palm down, in front of body, move them horizontally back and forth)
ALT-I-TUDE	(both hands pointed up, forefingers extended, moving upward)
and	
NEAR-NESS TO THE OCEAN	(imitate a swimmer doing the crawl stroke; hence the connection to the ocean)

Each year my students had trouble remembering the major factors that affect climate. Since latitude and altitude both rhyme and have the same number of syllables, this cadence came to mind—I could feel the rhythm of it. Originally, we clapped the syllables as we said the words. Later, movements were added, which cemented the meaning as well.

Subject Area: Mathematics

*The Integer Song (to the tune of "The Beverly Hillbillies")
Written by Margaret Fennessey's seventh grade students at George Fisher Middle School in Carmel, NY, 1996.

Addition
If the signs are the same, add and keep the sign.
If the signs are different, subtract and keep the sign of the
higher absolute value, OH BOY !
And that's what you do for addition
        Example: -8 + +5 = -3
                         -7 + -2 = -9

Subtraction
Stay, change, switch—is what you want to do,
When subtraction of integers is asked of you.
Follow the rules for addition after that,
And you'll have the answer down pat !
        Example: -5   -   -9   =   +4
                        (stays -5) (change to +) (switch to +9) =   +4
                              -5   +   +9   =   +4

Multiplication and Division
The rules are the same when you divide or multiply,
If the signs are the same, positive is the reply.
If the signs are different, negative is what you say,
And now you know all the rules today.
        Example: -14 ÷ -2   = +7
                       -3 × -4   = -12

Students found this to be a valuable study aid to recall the integer rules. Mrs. Fennessy told us each year several students are heard singing The Integer Song under their breath during a quiz! Now, each year, the students consistently do well with this concept.

*Are You Metric? (to the tune of "Frère Jacques")
From "If the Shoe Fits" (stanza one) then Jan added stanza two

Ten millimeters
Ten millimeters
Equals one centimeter
Equals one centimeter

You need ten millimeters
You need ten millimeters
To equal one centimeter.

One hundred centimeters
One hundred centimeters
Equals one meter
Equals one meter
You need one hundred centimeters
You need one hundred centimeters
To equal one meter.

*Denominator-Numerator
From Rappin' and Rhymin', *by Doctor Rosella Wallace, 1992. Used with permission of Zephyr Press, Chicago.*

SmartRope, SmartRope, what's the trick
To help me learn my arithmetic?
Denominator down—**touch the ground**.
Numerator top—**give a hop**.
SmartRope, SmartRope, fractions are neat.
Just remember to keep the beat.

Be sure to add body movements to the bolded words!

*The Measurement Song (to the tune of "Dem Bones")
Adapted by Amy and Jan from graduate students at the State University of New York at New Paltz

Two cups, two cups = one pint,
Two cups, two cups = one pint,
Two cups, two cups = one pint,
So measure out those pints.

Two pints, two pints = one quart,
Two pints, two pints = one quart,
Two pints, two pints = one quart,
So measure out those quarts.

Four quarts, four quarts = one gallon,
Four quarts, four quarts = one gallon,
Four quarts, four quarts = one gallon,
So measure out those gallons.

(Add hand motions to show increased sizes—choose your own motions)

*Music Fractions

This idea comes from Teaching K–8, February 2003

To enable students to feel and hear the meaning of fractions, beat out the number of parts in a whole by tapping desks with a pencil or stick (grades 2–4).

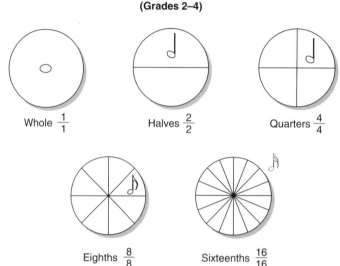

Beat Out the Meaning of Fractions

(Grades 2–4)

Whole $\frac{1}{1}$ Halves $\frac{2}{2}$ Quarters $\frac{4}{4}$

Eighths $\frac{8}{8}$ Sixteenths $\frac{16}{16}$

Musical notation is full of fractions, and examining beats within a measure of music is a great way to look at equivalent fractions and adding fractions once students can identify the note value (Grades 4–8).

Whole   Half   Quarter   Eighth   Sixteenth

In 4–4 time, four quarter notes make up one measure of music. Give your students a few bars of music, and ask them to write the note values as a fraction beneath each note. They should add up the fractions and see if they add up to exactly one.

For a challenge, include dotted notes, which are played for 50 percent longer than an undotted note. Ask your students to determine the values of dotted half, quarter, and eighth notes (the values are three-fourths, three-eighths, and three-sixteenths, respectively).

Finally, here's a fun problem: How many ways can eighth, quarter, half, and whole notes be arranged in 2–4, 4–4, or 6–8 measures? Consider only the duration of the notes; put no emphasis on the tunes. There are more combinations than you might think!

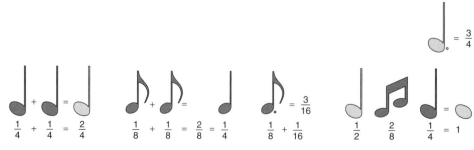

$= \frac{3}{4}$

$\frac{1}{4} + \frac{1}{4} = \frac{2}{4}$ $\frac{1}{8} + \frac{1}{8} = \frac{2}{8} = \frac{1}{4}$ $\frac{1}{8} + \frac{1}{16} = \frac{3}{16}$ $\frac{1}{2}$ $\frac{2}{8}$ $\frac{1}{4} = 1$

*It's the Operations Rap
Written by Amy Schwed and Janice Melichar-Utter

When you *add* two numbers,
The answer is the *sum*.
　　It's the *sum*,
　　It's the *sum*.

When you *add* two numbers,
They're both called *addends*.
　　Addend plus *addend*,
　　Addend plus *addend*.

When you *subtract* two numbers
The answer is the *difference*.
　　It's the *difference*.
　　It's the *difference*.

When you *subtract* two numbers,
The *minuend's* over the *subtrahend*.
　　Subtrahend's down below,
　　Subtrahend's down below.

When you *multiply* two numbers,
The answer is the *product*.
　　It's the *product*.
　　It's the *product*.

When you *multiply* two numbers,
The *multiplicand* goes on top.
　　The *multiplier* does the work,
　　The *multiplier* does the work.

When you *divide* two numbers,
The answer is the *quotient*.
　　It's the *quotient*.
　　It's the *quotient*.

When you *divide* two numbers,
The *divisor* goes into the *dividend*.
　　It's *divisor* into *dividend*,
　　It's *divisor* into *dividend*.

*Area and Perimeter Cheer
Written by Amy Schwed and Janice Melichar-Utter

Walk around the room with me
Take a step and you will see.
Perimeter is what we find
As we walk our way around the room.

(Walk around the room, repeating as needed.)

Feet, inches, centimeters,
Perimeter has many uses

To find the space that is inside
I'll take you on a different ride.
Area is what we use
To measure space that is inside.

(Walk around the middle of the room.)

Square feet, square inches, square centimeters,
Area has many different uses

So if you want to build a fence
Perimeter will make good sense.

And if it's carpet you must lay
Area will surely be the way.

The following are songs by Kay Aileen Smitherman (2005). Visit her Web site at www.mathsongs.com for books and CDs she has written.

*Old MacDonald's Polygon Barn (to the tune of "Old MacDonald Had a Farm")

Old MacDonald had a barn, full of polygons!
And in that barn a polygon, called a triangle.
Three sides here,
Three sides there,
Three-sided triangle.
Old MacDonald had a barn, full of polygons!

Old MacDonald had a barn, full of polygons.
And in that barn a polygon, that we call a square.
With four sides here
Just alike.
Here a square; there a square,
All the sides just alike.

Three sides here,
Three sides there,
Triangle, triangle,
Three-sided triangle,
Old MacDonald had a barn, full of polygons.

Old MacDonald had a barn, full of polygons.
And in that barn a polygon, called a rectangle.
With two short sides
And two long sides,
Short sides, long sides,
Call it a rectangle.

Four sides here
Just alike,
Here a square, there a square,
All the sides just alike.

Three sides here,
Three sides there,
Triangle, triangle,
Three-sided triangle.
Old MacDonald had a barn, full of polygons.

*Pyramid Volume for Bears (to the tune of "The Bear Went Over the Mountain" or "For He's A Jolly Good Fellow")

> To find a pyramid's volume,
> The rule for finding the volume
> Is find the area of the base . . .
> Times height. Divide by three.

*M–E–A–N (Sing as a "round" to the tune of "Row, Row, Row Your Boat")

> Mean: M–E–A–N
> Add the numbers, then
> Count the numbers and divide.
> Mean: M–E–A–N!

*Adding Decimals (Sing as a "round" to the tune of "Are You Sleeping?") (This is the last stanza and it tells it all.)

> When you're adding,
> Or subtracting,
> Line them up.
> Line them up.
> Line up all the decimals.
> Every number has one.
> Line them up.
> Line them up.

Subject Area: General Knowledge

*Old Faithfuls
> Remembering things:

- Thirty days hath September,
  April, June and November,
  All the rest have thirty-one
  Save February which has twenty-eight.

- Spring ahead, fall back

- Righty tighty, lefty loosey.

This one comes in handy when faced with opening a tight jar lid or turning on a faucet.

> **Now add your own!**

Another wonderful source is the "Schoolhouse Rock" songs and videos. They cover all content areas and can be used with a variety of grade levels. (www.school-house-rock.com)

*Studying a New Concept in Any Subject Area
Adapted from "If The Shoe Fits . . ." Carolyn Chapman

Again, divide your class into small groups (three or four is ideal). Each group needs to develop a song, rap, jingle, poem, or cheer to review a new concept. Naturally, all of the group members must take part in presenting their idea to the rest of the class.

- If a song is written, then it must use a tune that everyone knows.
- Use original words in whatever you create.
- Create visuals that will help the rest of the class learn from your product.
- When you are done, find a quiet place to practice your presentation.
- Finally, all groups will have an opportunity to share.

All age groups love this challenge.

> *"Music used in conjunction with a lesson can teach 60 percent of the content in 5 percent of the time of lessons taught without music."*
>
> —Eric Jensen

> *"Music is a gift. It will enrich your life and will always be your friend. When you hear a child singing to himself before he goes to sleep or humming as he builds his tower of blocks, you know that music is becoming his friend too."*
>
> —Jackie Silberg

> *"A vital part of the music, movement, and learning connection is the realization we are all songwriters."*
>
> —Hap Palmer

> *"Music is:*
>
> > *Bonding with nature*
> > *Allowing creativity to express itself*
> > *Refreshment of the spirit*
> > *A development of the spiritual within us*
> > *Getting in touch with eternal flow*
> > *Resurgence of self*
> > *Reconvening of life*
> > *Spiritual bonding*
> > *Involvement–an 'at-oneness' with the rhythm of living."*
>
> —Barbara Crowe,
> quoted in *Music: Physician for Times to Come* (Lazear, 2004)

Music Alone
All things must perish from under the sky;
Music alone shall live,
Music alone shall live,
Music alone shall live,
Never to die.

> —Traditional German

Anything learned with music will not be forgotten.

SUMMARY OF KEY CONCEPTS
IN THIS CHAPTER

- Be-Boppin' the Brain
  - What Experts Tell Us
  - Teaching Piggyback Songs
- Study Strategies in Language Arts
  - The Essay Boogie
  - BINGO Facts
  - The Period Song
  - Parts of Speech
  - Learn Spelling Words With Songs
  - Parts of Speech Song
  - The Contraction Song
  - *TH* Words Spelling Rap
  - City–Comma–State Punctuation Rap
  - Question Words Spelling Rap
  - Cheer
  - The Well-Known Spelling Rule
- Study Strategies in Science
  - Cerebellum Song
  - Decomposition Rap
  - Recycle Songs
  - Rock Rap
  - Butterfly Cycle
- Study Strategies in Social Studies
  - The Thirteen Colonies
  - Twinkle, Twinkle, Where We Are:
    A Song About the Continents
  - Factors Affecting Climate
- Study Strategies in Mathematics
  - The Integer Song
  - Are You Metric?
  - Denominator–Numerator
  - The Measurement Song
  - Music Fractions
  - It's the Operations Rap
  - Area and Perimeter Cheer
  - Old MacDonald's Polygon Barn
  - Pyramid Volume for Bears
  - M–E–A–N
  - Adding Decimals
- Study Strategies for General Knowledge
  - Old Faithfuls
  - Studying a New Concept in Any Subject Area

6

Talking Tightens Memory

Walking Down Verbal/ Linguistic Lane

" I got a thesaurus for Christmas. I was startled, stunned, taken aback, flabbergasted, mind-boggled, left open-mouthed, incredulous, nonplussed, struck with wonder, awestruck, confounded..."

Illustration by Bruce Wasserman

How many people would be thrilled to receive a thesaurus as a birthday gift? How would you feel about this gift? If you had strong verbal-linguistic intelligence, it would be a treasure!

A third-grade teacher, working on the reading skill of drawing conclusions, asked her students to read a chapter for homework and draw conclusions. One little girl in her class raised her hand and asked, "Is it okay if I type my conclusions? I don't really like to draw" (Haynes, 2006).

Verbal/Linguistic Background

Schools are built on a verbal/linguistic foundation. Learners who are not strong linguistically will struggle to grasp and remember new ideas communicated in text or lecture form. Helping students generate connections between the new information they are trying to process verbally with facts they already know is a challenge! Integrating learners' strengths with various language strategies gives learners additional pegs to attach ideas presented verbally. Writing provides tactile input and serves as a tool for refining thinking and cementing new learning. Debates and discussions rev up emotions, and strong emotions equal strong memory links. Mnemonics provide a framework to which new ideas are associated and enable new concepts to move into long-term memory.

This chapter presents many study techniques which provide elaborative rehearsal methods needed by all learners. These strategies tap into other student strengths to assist the acquisition of verbal/linguistic knowledge. In reality, many pathways converge and naturally support each other.

MNEMONICS

Mnemonics are techniques or tricks to memorize information. They generally have no meaningful connection to the facts that need to be learned, but provide an auditory or visual framework to cue the information into long term memory. Students enjoy their game-like approach to learning. The more outlandish the mnemonic, the more easily it's remembered. Personalizing the mnemonic sentences taps into students' emotions. This technique is most effective when developed by the students—not the teacher—and comes in two forms: acrostic sentences and acronyms.

Acrostic Sentences

You know the acronym HOMES for the *Great Lakes* (Huron, Ontario, Michigan, Erie, and Superior). Resource room fifth graders developed an acrostic sentence to remember the Great Lakes' locations from east to west:

Only **E**ric **H**as **M**y **S**uspenders.

....

And, to piggyback from that, teachers in our workshop created one to show the progression from west to east:

She **M**ade **H**arry **E**at **O**nions.

....

An acrostic sentence that is probably familiar to many readers as a framework for the order of the planets is:

My **V**ery **E**arnest **M**other **J**ust **S**erved **U**s **N**ine **P**ies.
(Mercury, Venus, Earth, etc.)

....

The classification of plants and animals can be remembered with:

Krakatoa **P**ositively **C**asts **O**ff **F**umes
(kingdom, phyllum, class, order, family)

....

In third grade, Jan learned to spell "geography" with an acrostic sentence she still remembers each time she writes the word.

George **E**ats **O**nions. **G**eorge **R**ode **A** **P**ig **H**ome **Y**esterday.

Silly? Maybe. But it still works! Remember—the more ridiculous, the better!

....

Here's another. To learn the spelling of "plankton," the cartoonist Chuck Close, made up the following story:

"**P**igs **L**eaping **A**round, **N**early **K**illing **T**en **O**ld **N**eighbors."

He then visualized that scene whenever he needed to spell the word on a test (McGill, 1987).

Acronyms

Some familiar acronyms may include:

- **ROY G. BIV**
  (red, orange, yellow, green, blue, indigo, violet—the colors of a rainbow from bottom to top)
- **NATO**
  (North Atlantic Treaty Organization)
- **UNICEF**
  (United Nations International Children's Emergency Fund)
- **LASER**
  (light amplification simulated emission radiation)
- **SCUBA**
  (self-contained underwater breathing apparatus)

How many of you have met Princess SOH–CAH–TOA? In high school, she helped Amy's husband remember:

Sine = **O**pposite over **H**ypotenuse
Cosine = **A**djacent over **H**ypotenuse
Tangent = **O**pposite over **A**djacent

- **McHALES**
  (mechanical, chemical, heat, atomic, light, electric, solar)
  (forms of energy)

Did you know that the **USA PATRIOT** Act is an acronym too? It stands for:

Uniting and **S**trengthening **A**merica by **P**roviding **A**ppropriate **T**ools **R**equired to **I**ntercept and **O**bstruct **T**errorism

Acronyms are valuable in memorizing map data, such as learning the provinces of Canada. Fifth-grade teachers discovered students had difficulty remembering such names as Saskatchewan and Manitoba, while at the same time locating them on a map. So "Basmo Q," our silly Canadian clown friend, was created. "Basmo Q" visits the three "News" and discovers the Pie! The letters in Basmo Q's name spell out the provinces of Canada moving from west to east. The three "News" remind us of Newfoundland, New Brunswick, and Nova Scotia (which in Latin is New Scotland). By twisting around the letters in Prince Edward Island, we get PIE, a visual that easily sticks in the brain. We're grateful to Basmo Q, because most students quickly and easily learned and remembered the Canadian provinces. In fact, older middle school students would stop in and ask, "Hey, are you going to use Basmo again this year?"

Figure 6.2 Meet "BASMO Q"

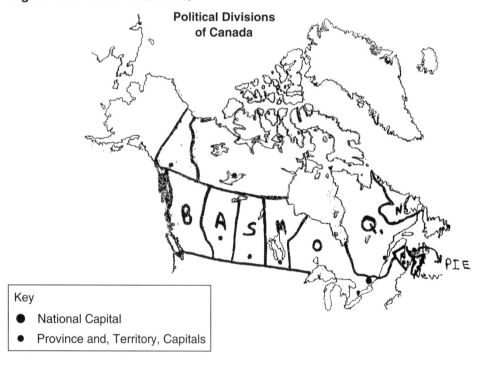

Political Divisions of Canada

Key

● National Capital

● Province and, Territory, Capitals

B - British Columbia
A - Alberta
S - Saskatchewan
M - Manitoba
O - Ontario
Q - Quebec

New - Newfoundland
New Brunswick
Nova Scotia
(Latin for New Scotland)

LECTURE AND TEXT NOTE TAKING

Do you remember being taught how to take notes? We don't! And neither do our children or grandchildren! Frequently students are left to figure out how to do this important skill on their own—and can't! Or, they do it poorly. How successfully can you study from notes if you don't know how to take good notes? How many students highlight almost every word, believing that everything is important? And, how do students know what is important?

Effective note taking is essential to studying successfully, writing accurate reports, and, ultimately, committing the learning to long-term memory. What makes notes effective? They must be clear, concise, accurate, not too wordy, and capture just the needed information. If you write down **everything**, it serves you poorly, as you can't determine what is really key. With that in mind, we recommend split page notes, a simplification of the Cornell note-taking method, with variations developed for different grade levels.

The first example of split page notes is at the primary level and has a strong visual component. The note-taking paper is folded in half. The left side gives the main idea, concept, or question, in picture format. The right side gives information gleaned from reading that explains the main idea, concept, or question posed. For primary grades, the teacher and students together select the key ideas to be listed and drawn on the left side and, by reading and discussing together, discern what facts need to be listed on the right side, under "What I've Learned". (See Figure 6.3.)

Figure 6.3 Noting What I've Learned

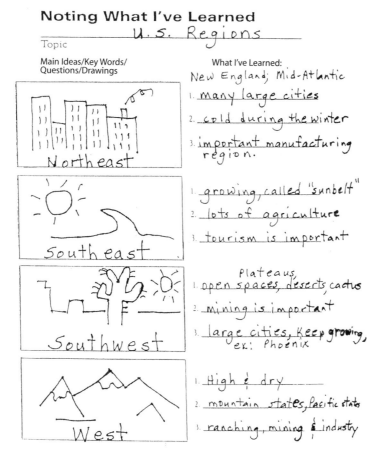

Upper primary and intermediate students might find the "Framed WH Words" format shown in Figure 6.4 useful with narrative text and newspaper articles. Here, the questions on the left are detail questions: who, what, where, when, why, and how, which are initially provided by the teacher. The right-hand side is used to record the answers found in the text. This format is also effective in teaching students to take notes from passages read aloud and is valuable in preparing students for standardized tests with a listening component. The goal is to have students set up this format on their own using blank paper. We suggest that students who struggle with spelling might prefer to draw pictures and words on the right side.

Figure 6.4 Framed WH Words

QUESTIONS	ANSWERS
WHO	Write answers or use drawings to record your ideas here.
WHAT	
WHERE	
WHEN	
WHY	
HOW	

An alternative is to replace questions with literary terms such as setting, characters, plot or problem, events, climax, or solution.

Intermediate grades and up will benefit from using the split page note-taking format in all subject areas (see Figure 6.5).

Information on the right side is not written in full sentences but rather in **short phrases**. It capsulizes the meaning of the text read, the video viewed, the Internet materials researched, or any source used, such as dictionary definitions. When the split page study notes are completed, work with the students to **highlight the key meaning words** in the right column. This forces the student to focus on the key words that become peg words for recalling information learned. This format becomes a study sheet when students cover the right column by folding the right edge of the paper to the vertical line at the end of the topic/question column. Students can review and memorize by covering and uncovering information as they study. When this information is confidently learned, students can now fold the left column of the paper, covering the topic/question, to further review what they are learning. This study strategy works well for many students, especially those who need many repetitions.

Figure 6.5 Split Page Notes (Study Sheet)

Topic/Questions	Details/Answers/Definitions

Stephen, a fifth-grade inclusion student, returned during seventh grade and excitedly entered the room with several disheveled sheets of binder paper in his hand. "Hey, Mrs. Melichar! I got a ninety-one on my science test! Wanna see my notes?" He showed me his split page notes, in large scribbly handwriting, organized just as I had taught him. If split-page notes worked so well for Stephen, they will work for anyone.

Students at the high school and college level will find the advanced split page notes, three column formats useful (see Figure 6.6).

Figure 6.6 Advanced Split Page Notes

ADVANCED SPLIT-PAGE NOTES		
Topics/Questions		Class Notes/Reflections

When teachers actively teach note taking, the moaning begins! This process of guiding students through the note-taking process is a challenging, time-consuming task. Many teachers bypass this, assuming previous teachers have taught note taking, and so simply state, "Read Chapter 2 and take notes," or, "Please take notes as we watch this video." Then comes the amazement! Teachers discover students are stumped; either they don't know what to write down so they copy everything, or they omit important information. Note taking needs to be taught, modeled, and **practiced together in class**.

Use the following steps to provide initial instruction in note taking skills:

1. Read text together, discussing key ideas and how you discerned them. Put these key ideas in note form on the board for students to copy.

2. Teach students to highlight. Photocopy a few pages from the text and read with the class. Discuss and pick out key ideas to be highlighted, and then connect important details that support the key ideas.

3. After the students and teachers have practiced note taking together, the following comparison practice helps students gain skill and confidence:

Give students an independent note-taking assignment, using either a short article or video. When students complete their notes, give them a copy of the teacher's notes to compare with their notes. Making the comparison is an added benefit. Discuss the notes recorded and why they were important. Note various styles, focusing on subtitles, wording of ideas, and the importance of not writing on every line. Leaving blank areas— white space—enables the brain to better see relationships and focus only on what's important. This activity needs to be repeated throughout the grades.

4. Another way to help structure the note-taking process is by using "skeletal" notes, containing the main (key) ideas of a lecture or text, organized into headings and subheadings. Skeletal notes provide a framework that enables students to see the text organizational pattern. Leave blank spaces between headings so students can record additional notes. This technique is effective at all grade levels, in all content areas, and is especially helpful to low-performing students who may have poor listening and note-taking skills (Gall, Gall, Jacobsen, & Bullock, 1990; see Figure 6.7). Partial webs can also be used to teach identifying the main idea and supporting details.

5. Teach students that the information a teacher writes on the board or presents via overhead or PowerPoint is important to record.

6. Teaching note taking is an arduous task but well worth it! The recorded notes are the information students study when reviewing or preparing for a test. Note taking is a life long skill and your students will return and thank you for teaching them when they're in college.

Figure 6.7 Skeleton Split Page Notes (Study Sheet Form)

Characteristics	**SHARKS**
	1. stream lined shape
	a. _____
	b. _____
	2. _____
	3. excellent smell
	4. teeth
	a. _____
	5. some lay eggs
	6. _____
	7. _____
Structure	1. small eyes
	2. _____
	3. _____
	4. _____
	5. very tough skin
Species	1. 200 different kinds
	2. _____
	3. _____
	4. _____
	5. _____
_____	1. dolphins
	2. _____
	3. whales
	4. _____
Food	1. squid
	2. crabs
	3. _____
	4. _____
	5. _____
	6. eats garbage
_____	1. for vitamins
	2.
	3. _____
	4. sport

Figure 6.8 Skeleton Shark Web

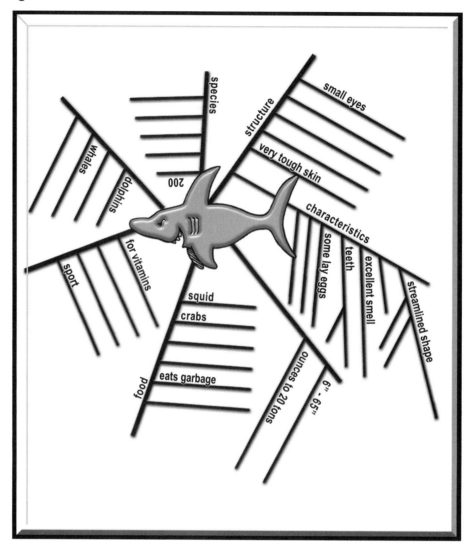

Illustration by Bruce Wasserman

Analyzing the Note-Taking Process

Let's look at some background information that creates awareness of three steps in the note-taking process:

   (a) **Observe**—noticing facts and relationships
   (b) **Record**—the note-taking process, and
   (c) **Review**—an integral part of note taking

Observe—Notice Facts and Relationships

The first thing students need to do is observe and be "mentally present" in class, which means to be alert, with no daydreaming.

- Pay attention.
- Think with the speaker, think of examples, and try to connect to your background.

- Think critically about what you hear.
- Let go of judgments about the teacher's style.
- Postpone debate; just record the facts.
- Accept your wandering mind—use the *checkmark system* to get back on track (see Chapter 11).
- Watch for clues, as they are hints about what notes are important and might show up on tests. Be alert for repetition.
- Listen for introductory, concluding, and transition words and phrases.
- Notice the teacher's interest level. This is a clue that the material is probably important.

Record—How to Write Notes

- Use split page format.
- Create mind maps and graphic organizers.
- Write notes in outline form.
- Use key words—limit notes to only main-meaning words.
- Use pictures and diagrams (remember "a picture's worth a thousand words").
- Copy material from the board, overhead, or PowerPoint presentation.
- Use a three-ring binder (for movement and addition of papers).
- Use only one side of the paper (to fold for studying).
- Use four by six or five by eight cards.
- Keep your own thoughts separate. Students might want a side column for their reactions to ideas.
- Use an "I'm lost" signal, such as a "?" if you don't understand something.
- Label, number, and date all notes.
- Use standard abbreviation.

b/c = because	b/f = before	* = important	w/o = without
w/ = with	+ = and	∴ = therefore	cont. = continue

- Use white space. Don't crowd notes.
- Use tape recorders for auditory review.
- Use complete sentences only when material is important or difficult.
- Use graphic symbols, such as asterisks or arrows.
- Add text page numbers to refer back.

Review—An Integral Step

The third and final step in note-taking is review. This is the step students tend to ignore, so teachers again need to model, by doing it together with the class. Without review, much of the benefit of note taking is lost since review paves the road to long-term memory.

- Reread and edit within twenty-four hours.
- Note key words in the right column in split page format.
- Conduct short weekly reviews to provide spaced reinforcement.

- Use key words as cues to recite; **speaking notes aloud** assists in moving information into long-term memory. Adding the auditory component to support the visual changes how the brain processes.
- Consider word-processing notes.
- Change notes into mind maps or graphic organizers, especially when the material is difficult.

Card Cramming

Here's a strategy that will motivate students to focus on preparing for a test. One or two weeks before a big test, announce to your students that they'll be able to use notes during the test as long as those notes fit on a standard five by seven index card, front and back if they wish. Hand out the cards and assure the students that, yes, they can write as small as they like, and yes, they can include anything that will help them ace the test: definitions, names, dates, formulas, diagrams, and so on. Just making the card forces students to think about the material and summarize it. Surprisingly, many of them may not even have to use the cards on the day of the test (Wormeli, 2005).

10–24–7

Jenny Severson, EdD, presented the Learning Forum's "Principle of 10–24–7" at the Learning Brain Expo, 2006. To transfer new learning to long-term memory, review initial learning within ten minutes, within twenty-four hours, and again in seven days. Initial review strategies Severson discussed were:

- Turn and talk to your neighbor about . . .
- Read over your notes and add a drawing for . . .
- Create a series of body movements for . . .
- Make review cards. (see Card Cramming)

Remember—If you don't use it, you'll lose it!

Figure 6.9 "If you don't use it, you lose it."

Illustration by Bruce Wasserman

BEM Principle

BEM stands for beginning, ending, and middle and is based on the Primacy-Recency Effect. "During a learning episode, we remember best that which comes first, second best that which comes last, and least that which comes just past the middle" (Sousa, 2001, p. 89). So, shorten lessons! In a forty-minute time period, teaching two twenty-minute lessons provides 20 percent more prime time than one forty-minute lesson. The idea is to make more beginnings and endings, thereby eliminating the middle time, when students don't pay attention. Lessons divided into twenty-minute segments are more productive than one continuous lesson. Teachers need to arrange short breaks; lead students in a short group activity or a "stand and stretch" think-pair-share activity or TTYPAS. These are explained in the next section (Cafarella, as cited in Sousa, 2001).

During study time the greater amount of attention and rehearsal is allocated to the first few items being studied. So, sometimes begin your studying at the end of your notes and the next day, begin in the middle. Simply changing where you start will assure all information is mastered.

Be sure to take study breaks. Just before and just after you take a break, your memory for an item is better. If you don't take a break, you will learn less in a given period of time. So don't push through your study. Take a break, and when you return, you will learn more effectively. When you take a break, do something different—go for a walk, do light exercise, stretch, have a snack or listen to music, anything—**as long as it is not watching TV**. Another hint is to study your weakest topic first or after a break when you are freshest (Recall Plus, 2004).

Research Note Taking

More challenges arise when students go to the library or Internet for research. This requires another set of skills. And, once again, it is the responsibility of the teacher to teach, model, and practice these new skills. When researching, there are four basic types of notes: (a) direct quotations, (b) paraphrasing, (c) summarizing, and (d) commenting.

Direct quotes are used when information is copied word for word from a source. Quotation marks are required and the source must be documented. Use direct quotes only when exact wording is memorable or of historic significance. Source attribution is a *must* to avoid plagiarism.

Paraphrasing is when ideas are written in your own words. Use it when ideas, but not exact words, are important.

Summarizing is stating the main idea of a long paragraph. Find the topic sentence in the paragraph and write briefly; complete sentences are not needed.

Comments give personal opinions about the information. They help reach conclusions and move the data into long-term memory.

Tips for research note taking:
- Use index cards
- Put only one idea or question on each card
- Put the source and page number on each card
- Put a brief heading at the top
- Leave room at the bottom for comments
- Keep a separate page for bibliographic information

Model, model, model . . . everything you teach! Your students will thank you. If a student is confused about an issue, he or she will go back to your modeling examples, which will provide more clarification than an explanation would.

STUDY STRATEGIES FOR ALL CONTENT AREAS

Talk, Talk, Talk

Talking and discussion are effective ways to do elaborative rehearsal. Students delve into any content more profoundly when there is a conversation, debate, or decision to make.

1. Think-Pair-Share/TTYPAS

Spencer Kagan (1994) recommended Think-Pair-Share, developed by Professor Frank Lyman, University of Maryland Howard County Southern Teacher Education Center, MD. First, a problem is posed or a question is asked. Students are given time to think alone for a specified amount of time. Then pairs are formed to discuss the problem or question. Finally, they share their answer or thoughts with the class.

According to Kagan, when you substitute a team discussion for the last step of Think-Pair-Share, a very different structure is created. When students discuss the topic within their teams there may be eight times as much participation (Kagan, 1994).

These are some sample discussion items:

- Think about just one word that sums up what we've been talking about. Give reasons for your choice.
- Take two to three minutes to draw what you have learned and share with your partner.
- Create a series of body motions to demonstrate.
- Explain how the new learning makes sense and relates to your life.
- Recall the main points. (Specify a number if you wish.)
- Predict what will be presented next.
- Discuss how the learning is similar to something you already know. (Create a simile, metaphor, or analogy.)

A variation on Think-Pair-Share is "T.T.Y.P.A.S." which is "Turn To Your Partner And Share." This is a simple, informal interactive strategy that teachers can use as a "pause and think" time during a longer discussion, lecture, film, and so on. It signals the brain to tune in and think by creating a need for dialogue. Then the outer thinking becomes inner thinking (Fogarty, 1997, as cited in Weaver and Cortell, 1986). Now, an open highway to long-term memory has been established.

2. Debates and Conversations

Debates and conversations get students to both think and talk about concepts they have learned. Role-playing and personifications are two fun ways to do this. These might involve writing or could be done extemporaneously. In all cases, debates and conversations review concepts learned and require students to think about them in different ways and with different points of view.

In social studies, ask students to develop conversations or topical debates between:

- people living in different historical periods
- people from different political parties or with different points of view, such as farmers and ranchers or ecologists and businessmen
- people from different levels of society

In science, ask students to develop conversations or topical debates between:

- two organs in the body, such as the liver and the mouth, or bones and muscles
- two chemical elements
- various types of simple machines such as a block and tackle talking to a lever

In math, ask students to develop conversations or topical debates between:

- a plus sign and a multiplication sign
- a fraction and a percent
- a triangle and a square
- a meter stick and a yard stick

In reading/language arts, ask students to develop conversations or topical debates between:

- any two parts of speech, such as a subject and a verb
- any two punctuation marks, such as an exclamation mark and a period
- any two characters in a book

These are just a few ways to generate elaborative rehearsals and motivate higher-level thinking using Bloom's Taxonomy. Students will be stimulated as they transfer information into their memory banks.

3. Decisions, Decisions

Literary characters often have problems to be solved or decisions to be made.

a. Direct students to list all the decisions a character faced in a story or book.
b. Then select the one decision they feel was most important and defend why it was chosen. Be sure to consider the consequences of each decision as it leads students to dig into all aspects of a book.

Students develop in-depth understanding through personifications, problems and solutions, and comparisons. These elaborative rehearsal strategies, whether spoken or written, imbed new learning firmly into memory, and students will not forget the **fun** they had with these discussions.

4. Literary Memory Pegs

Historically, cultures placed a high value on stories, poems, and myths in order to preserve their history and traditions. Likewise, students can weave new vocabulary and concepts of any content area into poems, short stories, pourquoi tales or myths. Information that is organized with emotional coloring is more easily remembered and retrieved than random facts, and writing evokes, stimulates, and develops the imagination.

> Small groups research and list facts and key concepts or use lecture and textbook notes.
> Choose and highlight both key vocabulary and concepts.
> Students write a creative piece, using each of the key vocabulary and concepts identified.

Here's a science example using water cycle vocabulary words: *evaporation, condensation, precipitation, collection, transpiration,* and *ground water.*

It's raining, it's snowing.
Precipitation's growing.

Lakes get fuller; **ground water** deepens.
Earth's water **collection** is forever seepin'.

Plants **transpire**; humans perspire.
Evaporation sends water to clouds up higher.

When moist, vapory clouds meet cold air.
Condensation makes rain somewhere.

Although the story or poem that is composed is not necessarily quality writing, the process of manipulating and playing with the vocabulary and key ideas generates new memory pegs to transfer information into long-term memory. Once again, it is the **process** that is the important step in stimulating the dendrites to make new connections.

Myths are especially adaptable to the science curriculum and stories can be used to remember math processes, especially related to word problems. Write poems describing when to use different math operations. They will help students solve word problems.

5. "Thirty Seconds Please"

Objective:
* Students will do a comprehensive review of all significant information in any unit of study.

Activity:

1. The teacher needs a stop watch to time thirty seconds and individual slips of paper with one topic written on each slip—a key vocabulary/topic/important person or event from a unit of study (at least one per student.) Place papers in a bag. In a second bag, place numbered pieces of paper, one for each student.

2. Teacher and students arrange themselves in a circle.

3. Students choose one paper from each bag. Give students a minute of think time to decide what they want to say about the topic selected.

4. In round one, the students each speak about their topic for thirty seconds. Teacher times them.

5. Teacher lists each topic on the board as it is presented.

6. In round two, the student who chose number one goes first. She or he chooses a topic that someone else spoke about in round one, tells the significance of the topic to the unit, and adds important information not given. Student number two goes second, and so forth. Do not time this round.

7. Other students or the teacher may add tidbits that further elaborate.

8. Encourage students to take notes on any information they feel they need to review.

This activity can be adapted to a novel. Students will select an important noun related to the book from a bag. During round one, each student will speak for thirty seconds telling his or her personal experience or knowledge about the noun. In round two, the student will tell the direct significance of the noun in the story. What a FUN way to review!

With thanks to Kelli Trevorah, graduate student SUNY New Paltz

"Words are a vehicle carrying concepts into the storeroom of one's memory."

"Good notes are your insurance against forgetting."

—Bragstad & Stumpf

SUMMARY OF KEY CONCEPTS IN THIS CHAPTER:

- Verbal/linguistic background
- Mnemonics
    - Acrostic Sentences
    - Acronyms
- Lecture and Text Note Taking
    - Split Page Notes—Study Sheet Forms
    - Analyzing the Process
        - Observe—Notice Facts and Relationships
        - Record—How to Write Notes
        - Review—An Integral Step
        - Card Cramming
        - 10–24–7

–BEM Principle
–Research Note Taking
- Study Strategies for All Content Areas
  –Talk, Talk, Talk
  –Think–Pair–Share/TTYPA
  –Debates and Conversations
  –Decisions, Decisions
  –Literary Memory Pegs
  –"Thirty Seconds Please"

7

Pumping Up Memory With Muscles

Running on the Body/Kinesthetic Track

Think of students you know who have trouble sitting still. Most classrooms have a number of these kinesthetically oriented students, yet the majority of our traditional classroom activities focus primarily on the verbal or analytical. Including kinesthetic study activities can give students a two-way information highway that is often neglected, and it **benefits *all* students!**

NANCY   **by Jerry Scott**

Nancy © United Feature Syndicate, Inc..

Look at Nancy in this cartoon above. Her little "in room field trip" made all the difference in being able to go back to work easily.

BODY/KINESTHETIC BENEFITS

Body/kinesthetic activities serve many functions:

- They resemble activities **students would do themselves** if not in school.
- They offer **more sensory input** and students tend to retain more learning.
- They promote **deeper processing, producing long-term** muscle memory rather than **short-term recall**.
- They enhance memory, learning, attention, decision-making, and multi-tasking, among other mental functions (Roan, 2006).

We need to guide students in using all modalities simultaneously. For example, when a student looks at information being studied (visual intake), reads it orally, (auditory input), and uses movements to feel the muscular symbolic representations of information (kinesthetic stimulus), input is entered using three key senses. Studies show that the brain performs best when the blood is flushed with oxygen, as it is when moving or exercising. This paves the road to learning for a smooth ride into long-term memory.

Movement, in general, enables students to be more engaged in learning and enhances memory. One parent reported that as she helped her son study for a test, they walked around the kitchen table, walking and talking about the subject matter simultaneously. He did extremely well on that test!

Levinson and Sanders (1992), in their book *Turning Around the Upside Down Kids*, stated:

> Dyslexic athletes often reported to Dr. Levinson that they were able to read and concentrate better when they were training for baseball or basketball or football. Other scientists noted the same thing and began recommending sports exercises and gymnastics to help kids that were learning disabled as well as those who were klutzy. The exercise helps their brains' fine tuners and so the visual and hearing inputs as well as the motor outputs get better. (p. 148).

The same results may be achieved by horseback riding, running, martial arts, and so forth.

Sit in any college library and watch students deeply engrossed in their reading. Some of them will be bouncing one foot up and down. Although it may drive other students crazy, the leg-jittering student is more focused and alert because of this movement.

As a general aid to body/kinesthetic learners, we would like to suggest the following study tips:

- Exercise while thinking through information or developing a thought.
- Have something to squeeze or hold, such as a Koosh ball, a piece of clay, or so forth.

- Skip, jump, clap, and hop while studying at home.
- Wiggle your toes inside your shoes—it won't disturb anyone next to you.
- Take a short study break to exercise: do isometrics, push-ups, cross-laterals—whatever works for you (see Chapter 4).
- Twiddle your thumbs or tap a pencil (quietly, *on your leg*).
- Recopy your notes by hand or key them into a computer.
- Connect ideas to physical movements.
- Write ideas on index cards or Post-It notes; manipulate the order in a meaningful way.
- Write or doodle while listening; the actual movement in writing or drawing helps you to focus.

The remainder of this chapter will present ready-to-use, teacher-tested study strategies utilizing body/kinesthetics. Some are content specific, but others are applicable in many areas. Use your imagination and adapt them to your needs.

Study Strategies in Body/Kinesthetics

A fifth-grade teacher had been directing her students in studying with actions. Students had fun sharing the motions and antics (no sounds allowed) they'd come up with to help remember vocabulary words or concepts.

Several days later, one special needs student, whose performance was erratic, did exceptionally well on a quiz. The teacher commented on his paper, "I can see you studied! I am proud of you." Quiz papers were sent home for parent signatures, as usual.

The next day, the teacher received a phone call from this student's mother. "What do you mean by, 'I can see you studied'? I know he *didn't* study."

The teacher suggested, "Why don't you ask your son about it?" And she did. The mother called back after a conversation with her son and happily reported that her son had, indeed, studied. In the privacy of his room, he had practiced all the actions for the vocabulary quiz.

For this student, as for many, studying with movement was an effective strategy.

LANGUAGE ARTS STUDY STRATEGIES

1. Act the Word

Objective: Use body movement to understand and move vocabulary words from any content area into long-term memory.

Activity:
- Assign cooperative groups of three:
  - Actors: Each member of the group is an actor.
  - Coach: Makes sure all group members know the words being studied.
  - Director: Announces the words and decides the order in which the words will be studied.
- The director shows the words.
- Each member reviews the word meaning and decides on the best action(s) to teach the word to the group. Do actions without any sounds.
- Then members take turns teaching their action(s) to the group. As a word is taught, all members do the motion while saying the word and the meaning over and over.
- The coach has each member review the words and their movement(s) for a final check.
- The cooperative groups come together. The class stands in a circle. The teacher calls out a word and the students do the action(s) they learned while saying the word and the meaning.
- The teacher may lead discussions to show how different actions can relate the meaning in different ways.

*Adapted from *If the Shoe Fits* by Carolyn Chapman (1993)

2. Punctuation: Sounds and Actions

Objective: To demonstrate understanding of various punctuation marks and where they belong in a sentence, using the body and sounds.

Activity:
- For each punctuation mark, the class can decide on a specific movement and an appropriately goofy sound to represent that mark. Some examples are as follows:
  - A period, for example, can be represented by punching a fist forward and saying, "Pow."
  - Two fingers pointing with two sounds like "phutt, phutt" can signal a colon.
  - Of course, an exclamation point could be made by raising both arms overhead and saying in an excited voice, "Aha!"
  - To show quotation marks, raise both arms, bend the index and middle fingers of both hands forward, while saying, "Boiing, boiing." Naturally, you can come up with motions and sounds for the other punctuation marks.

- Once the class is comfortable with all these sounds, they can chant unpunctuated passages, supplying the necessary punctuation gestures and sounds. There will be lots of laughs, and plenty of effective punctuation review. This activity is very Victor Borge-esque!
- Here's a more active variation of this activity. Tape oversized punctuation marks onto the chests of students. Each student is asked to decide on an appropriate way of impersonating that particular punctuation mark. As a passage is read aloud, the "punctuation people" jump up as needed.

This concept is easily adaptable to learning the four different types of sentences: (a) declarative (telling), (b) interrogative (asking), (c) exclamatory (showing feeling), and (d) imperative (commanding).

3. Feel the Vowel Spelling

Objective: Students will learn the spelling of selected words by reciting consonants and representing the vowels with their bodies.
Activity:

This spelling activity provides students with an alternate way to study for their weekly spelling tests. They use their bodies to act out and feel the vowels and their voices to name the consonants. Since students struggle most with the auditory discrimination of vowel sounds and their many variations, this activity uses muscle movement to provide another way to connect spelling and letter sequence into long-term memory.

- Provide each student with a copy of the following chart and post a large chart on the classroom wall.

Feel the Vowels!
Say the names of the consonants and act out the vowels.

> **A**-Raise both arms overhead with fingertips touching to form the top of the letter **A**.
> **E**–Use both hands to form **E**. The index finger and thumb form top and bottom lines of the letter and the other hand's index finger forms the middle line.
> **I**–Point to one eye.
> **O**–Point to your mouth and shape it like an **O**.
> **U**–Point to another person (you)—or, shape your index finger and thumb into the letter **U**.

- The teacher writes the spelling word on the chalk board; for example: *weather*
- Then spell it out:
    - –Students say the letter *w*.
    - –Students use both hands to form the letter *e*.
    - –Students raise both arms overhead to form *a*.
    - –Students say the letters *t* and *h*.
    - –Students use both hands to form the letter *e*.
    - –Students say the letter *r*.

Students say the word, and in this case, add the definition, because it's a homonym:

"Weather—the climate we have each day: sun, rain, snow, and fog."

- A second example: Write the word *issue* on the chalkboard.
  - –Students point to one eye.
  - –Students say, "Ess, ess."
  - –Students point to another student.
  - –Students use both hands to form the letter *e*.
  - –Students say the word.
- Demonstrate the procedure with the class and practice it together. Repeat each word three to five times. Share the procedure with parents so students are supported in using it at home.

4. Get Physical With Spelling

Objective: Students will remember specific letter orders or consonant-vowel patterns through actively using manipulatives or creative body movements (Barsch, 1974).
Activity:

- Spell the word out loud while bouncing a ball (or skipping rope) one time for each successive letter.
- Spell the word out loud while standing up whenever a consonant appears, and sitting down whenever a vowel appears (any two physical movements could be substituted for standing and sitting; Armstrong, 2003).

5. Walking the Review Path

Objective: Students will walk a brown Kraft paper path with drawn or glued symbols on the path to recall information to be learned. (It is more valuable when students draw or select the symbols themselves.)
Activity:

- Put any science, social studies, or math information in this format for students to walk and review. Use the Kraft paper lengthwise. Number each step and have a corresponding card with answers and explanations for review and recall of concepts. The "itchy" students, at any grade level, will benefit from the movement opportunity, which, in turn, enables them to focus, concentrate, and remember. Have students remove their shoes when walking the study path to recall.
- Students can work in pairs or small groups to prepare a review path. Groups can trade paths for extra practice.
- Laminate for protection.

Alternative:
Teacher writes out an entire story on a roll of Kraft paper. A predicable, patterned book containing sight words works well with this activity. The story goes from the bottom of the paper to the top. Allow space for the students to

illustrate the text. It's a little like walking up a paper ladder. The teacher reads the book several times with the students for familiarization, and then students illustrate each page.

Children take turns walking the story, reading each page as they go. They can also walk and read with a buddy.

6. Do It With Dance

Objective: To interpret a book or difficult concept with dance and music.
Activity:

- Examine the five main forms of dance—(a) ballet, (b) ethnic, (c) tap, (d) modern, and (e) jazz—for the differences in style. Modern and jazz have natural movement and flexibility. Ethnic is based on the cultures of other lands and helps us understand other nations. Ballet is characterized by graceful movements. Tap focuses on rhythmic clicking sounds. Dance provides discipline, endurance, and rhythmical coordination of mind and body.
- First, decide which style of dance represents your book or content. Is it lyrical like ballet? Is it peppy like tap? Is it filled with flexible movement like modern and jazz?
- Next, find a piece of music or parts of several musical compositions that fit the mood of the material.
- Finally, choreograph a musically accompanied dance that interprets the material and perform it.

One of Amy's sixth-grade students did a masterful job of portraying the life of Jonathan, the seagull in *Jonathan Livingston Seagull*, using various taped snippets of classical music and her ballet background, to dance and depict each stage of Jonathan's learning. Christine felt she would never forget this book because she choreographed and danced its highlights.

*Adapted from *Blast Off with Book Reports* by Debbie Robertson (1985)

7. A Friendly Letter

Objective: Demonstrate the parts of a friendly letter using the body.
Activity:

- Display a sample friendly letter, with each part clearly labeled: heading, greeting, body, closing, and signature.
- Ask students to stand beside their desks. Demonstrate how to use their bodies to recall the parts of a letter:
  –The heading is at the top —*Touch the top of your head.*
  –Next is the greeting—*Touch your mouth, say "hello."*
  –Then the body—*Twist your body.*
  –After that, the closing—*Touch your feet.*
  –Finally, the signature—*Imagine you have a pencil between your toes. Wiggle your toes as if you're signing your name.*

Each time the class needs to write a letter, have students stand and use their bodies to review the letter format.

Alternative:

When teaching the business letter format, alter the greeting. Teach students to greet a knight and say, *"Dear Sir Colon:" to remind students that they use "Sir" and a colon in this format.*

SOCIAL STUDIES STUDY STRATEGIES

1. Body Geography

Objective: To demonstrate knowledge of map directions and latitude lines by relating locations to the human body.

Activity:

- Students stand beside their desks, facing the front of the room. Hang a large United States map in front of students. Tell students, "If you were a building, point to where the roof would be." (Put hands on the top of the head.) Point out that the top of a map is **north**. Tell students, "If you were a building, point to where the foundation or basement is located." (Tap feet on the floor.) Point out that the bottom of a map is **south**, when facing the map. Ask students to stretch their arms out to the side and remind them that **west** is their left hand and **east** is their right hand. Practice by asking students to wave their west hand, and then wave their east hand. Use the word **"WE"** to remember that west is on the left and east is on the right when we look at a map.
- Still standing, with arms outstretched, look at a map of the United States and name states that belong to the left hand (west coast). Name states that belong to the right hand (east coast). Tell students to put their hands on their stomachs and name states that are at their middle (central states, the wheat growers, known as the "breadbasket"). Have students touch their heads and name states that go across the top (north) and then stamp their feet and name the states that go across the bottom (south).
- Relate map directions to the points on a compass rose.
- Repeat the activity using the intermediate points on the compass rose: NE, SW, NW, and SE.
- This activity can be used with latitude and longitude lines.

Figure 7.2 Compass Rose

Illustration by Bruce Wasserman

Figure 7.3 Globe, With Lines of Latitude.

Lines of Latitude

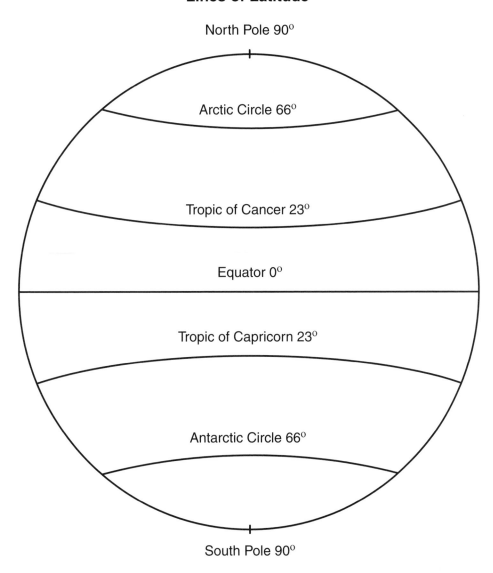

North Pole 90⁰

Arctic Circle 66⁰

Tropic of Cancer 23⁰

Equator 0⁰

Tropic of Capricorn 23⁰

Antarctic Circle 66⁰

South Pole 90⁰

- Give students the following body relationship hints to learn latitude lines. Some are so outlandish that they will certainly stick in their memories! Students stand and do the following motions as directed while naming the latitude lines.

  –North Pole—*Touch the top of the head, which is the northernmost point of the earth* (90 degrees N).

  –Arctic Circle—*Touch the sinus area of the head, where colds can settle and the climate is frigid* (66 degrees N).

  –Tropic of Cancer—*Touch the lower part of the lungs, where smokers can get cancer* (23⅓ degrees N).

  –Equator—*Put hands on waist, the middle of the earth and the middle of your body* (0 degrees).

  –Tropic of Capricorn—*Put hands on knee**caps*** (23⅓ degrees S).

  –Antarctic Circle—*Pretend to pull on boots, as warm boots are needed here* (66 degrees S).

–South Pole—*Stamp feet! It's the southernmost point of the earth, the location of Antarctica, and we're stomping on the "ants"* (90 degrees S).

–Later, add the prime meridian salute. *With the right hand in "salute" position, run this hand down the center of the body from the nose, over the navel, to the toes* (0 degrees longitude).

Figure 7.4 Picture of Boy With Corresponding Latitude Lines, Showing the Prime Meridian.

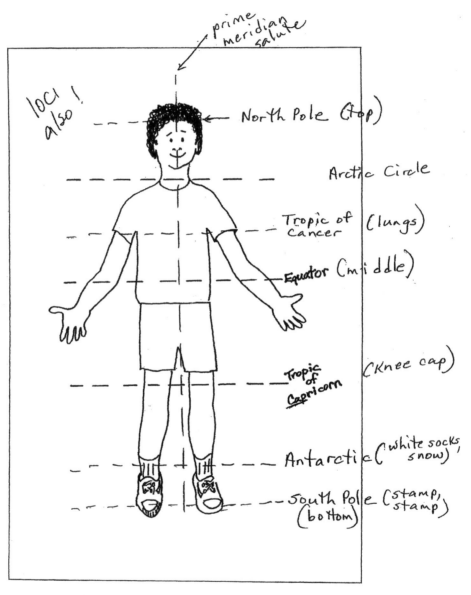

2. Latitude and Longitude Grid

Objective: To demonstrate knowledge of latitude and longitude by using a floor grid to locate various points.

Activity:

- Begin with an introduction on hemispheres and the main line of latitude (the equator) and the main line of longitude (the prime meridian) on a globe.

- Demonstrate hemispheres with oranges that represent the globe. Cut one on the equator to show the northern and southern hemispheres. Cut the other on the prime meridian to show the eastern and western hemispheres.
- Use a world map to show the two sets of lines that map makers put over maps and globes to make it easier to find various locations.
- Lines of latitude will be discussed and compared to a **ladder**. Like the steps of a ladder, lines of latitude run east to west, but to use the ladder, you go up and down, since lines of latitude measure distance north and south of the equator in degrees.
- Lines of **long**itude will be discussed, using the saying, "It's a **long, long** way from pole to pole." However, make sure students understand it is still 360 degrees around the world.
- A large, plastic floor grid marked off in latitude and longitude lines is placed in the middle of the room. (See Appendix for directions to make the grid.) Place a card with N and an up arrow at the top of the grid. Teach students that each line on the grid represents ten degrees.
- To introduce the students to the grid, have them remove their shoes; then teacher gives the following directions:
  - –All boys carefully walk onto the grid and stand in the northern hemisphere; all girls walk onto the grid and stand in the southern hemisphere.
  - –Everybody move to the western hemisphere.
  - –Girls, go to the eastern hemisphere.
  - –Everyone wearing navy blue, go to the southeast hemisphere.
  - –Everyone wearing red, stand on 0 degrees latitude. What do we call this line?
  - –Everyone with white socks, stand on 0 degrees longitude. What do we call this line?
  - –Girls, stand on the line that represents 50 degrees south. Boys, stand on the line that represents 30 degrees east. Teach the class that the place where the boys' and girls' lines intersect is known as 50 degrees south, 30 degrees east.

Now you have laid the foundation to understand how the grid lines help people find locations.

In the following activities, use a model ship and airplane because pilots and sailors need to rely on longitude and latitude lines for navigation.

- Students will sit around the outside of the grid with their shoes off and the teacher will place the model boat or airplane on a certain point. The teacher will then model how to find and write the latitude/longitude coordinates for that point. Always do latitude first, then longitude. Demonstrate two or three times.
- Two students work together to identify the model's coordinates by walking from the equator and the prime meridian to the model while counting the degrees of latitude and longitude aloud. The

pair calls out the location and classmates respond with "thumbs up" (correct) or "thumbs down" (incorrect). The teacher confirms and corrects, if necessary. These students then place a model at a new location. Repeat this process with the next two students until the entire class has had a turn. At some point in these activities, introduce the concept of five degrees if students don't do this on their own.

- A student will be asked to call out a location and a pair of students will place a model at that location. Again, use "thumbs up/down" to confirm correctness. Repeat until everyone has had a turn.
- Challenge students to tell you where they would be if they were standing on 0 degrees latitude and 0 degrees longitude.
- Ask them to stand on the location of their town. Research this together. Use a world map and find the answers!
- Have the students find the latitude and longitude for major world cities, such as London, New York, Athens, and Hong Kong. Locate them on the grid.
- Now provide similar activities on a paper grid.

The game "Battleship" practices similar brain patterning for students needing additional practice.

Variation: Yarn Maps

- Provide each student with a laminated world map that has lines of latitude and longitude drawn on it (30 degrees apart). See Appendix. Supply students with two different colored pieces of yarn, to act as lines of latitude and longitude.
- Students will use what they learned with the floor grid to find coordinates on the various continents, placing their yarn in the appropriate places. The coordinates for North America on the world map provided are 60 degrees north and 120 degrees west. Write down the coordinates for Bolivia, South America, Switzerland, Europe, and so forth; or give the coordinates for a point on an ocean, such as 0 degrees latitude and 0 degrees longitude. Ask the students to identify the ocean this coordinate is in and its approximate location.

*Variation thanks to Jennifer Capozzi, graduate student, SUNY New Paltz

3. Egyptian Social Pyramid

Objective: Students will demonstrate how the Egyptian social pyramid is constructed.

Activity:

- This is to be done after having read information about the Egyptian social system and having discussed the major concepts in a text.
- Students will create their own human Egyptian social pyramid. Begin by asking the class, "Who is on the top of the pyramid?" The person who answers, "The pharaoh" is given an index card labeled

"pharaoh" and stands in the front of the room as the "top" of the pyramid, holding up the card. (Note that there is only one student because there is only one pharaoh.) Continue this process by asking, "Who is next in line after the pharaoh?" When students answer, "Government officials," two students are each given an index card labeled "government officials," and they will stand in front of the pharaoh, holding up their cards. This procedure continues until the entire class forms the Egyptian social pyramid. The pyramid was created using a class of thirty students. The resulting human pyramid looked like this:

Figure 7.5 Human Pyramid

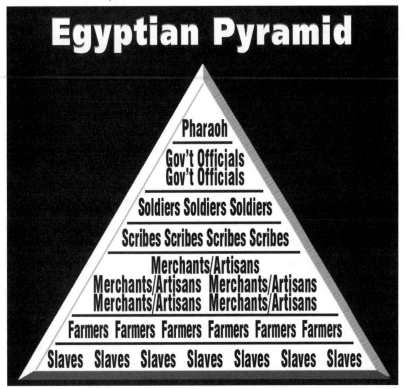

Illustration by Bruce Wasserman

This process will really cement these concepts into long-term memory. Once the pyramid is completed, discuss the following ideas:

- What role does the pharaoh play in the social pyramid?
- What is the role of the merchants and artisans? (Note that in the actual social pyramid, merchants are above the artisans, but in this pyramid, they had to be combined for numbers purposes. Review this with the students.)
- How important are farmers to the Egyptian society? Why?
- Why are the slaves on the bottom of the pyramid? What role do they play in Egyptian society?
- How would an Egyptian change his social position?
- How does this compare to our social system today?

Variation:

Have students each randomly draw cards representing each social stratum in Egyptian society (as shown in Figure 7.5). Then they will look at their cards and decide where they think they fit within the pyramid. Who should be on the top of the social system? ("The pharaoh.") Who is next in line after the Pharaoh? ("Government officials.") Continue with the rest of the people to physically form the social pyramid. Discussions will ensue as to the correct order of soldiers, scribes, merchant, artisans, and so forth. Students can be directed back to materials previously read to prove the correct order.

*With thanks to Leigh Flood-Legare, graduate student, SUNY New Paltz

4. Land Form Charades

Objective: Students will work in groups using colored paper and body movements to act out the land forms being studied, moving land form definitions, and visualizations into long-term memory.

Activity:
- Place students in groups of four or five.
- Give each group the following sheets of construction paper:

  3 blue—symbolizing water
  2 green—symbolizing lowlands and wetlands
  1 yellow—symbolizing higher flat lands
  1 orange—symbolizing highlands and plateaus
  1 brown—symbolizing mountains of high elevation

  (Note: These colors follow the topography key on most graphic relief maps.)

- Each group selects one land form name printed on a card from the "grab-bag" the teacher has prepared. The groups are given two to three minutes to think out how they will present their land form to the class using only actions and their colored paper. (Model how this can be done with the examples below.) No words or sounds may be used. Remind them to work quietly as they plan, so others in the class do not overhear what they are planning.

For example, a **mountain** may be acted out by having each student in the group stand in a circle or oval, facing each other, with their hands overhead, holding strips of brown paper that touch each other. A **river** may be acted out by having two students holding green paper stand about five feet apart, facing each other (river banks). The remaining students carry blue paper and walk between the banks, moving in the same direction (flow of water).

- As the land form charade is presented, each group writes on paper what land form they think it represents. This keeps everyone actively involved and it enables the teacher to keep score, if desired.

It is amazing how creatively students use their bodies to represent the various land forms.

SCIENCE STUDY STRATEGIES

1. Ecosystems

Objective: Students will demonstrate an understanding of the interdependence of animals, people, and plants in a rainforest by participating in an ecosystem simulation.

Activity:

- Prepare necktie cards in advance by putting a long piece of string through two holes in an index card so that the cards can be hung around each student's neck. Each card will have the name of a rainforest animal printed on it. Prepare a yardstick with long pieces of yarn attached to it, to act as the Kapok Tree. There needs to be one piece of yarn for each student.
- Read *The Great Kapok Tree* by Lynn Cherry (1990), asking students to pay particular attention to all the different animals that need the Kapok Tree. Discuss how all the animals rely on the tree. Define and discuss the Kapok Tree as an ecosystem.
- Give each student a necktie card with a different animal from the book's ecosystem on it. These cards are worn by the students while doing the simulation. You may have to double up on some of the animals. Select one student to hold up the Kapok Tree yardstick.
- Have the students form a circle. Place the Kapok Tree in the center, holding the yardstick with all the pieces of yarn attached to it. Now, reread the book. When the student hears his or her animal, the student will go to the Kapok Tree, take and hold one piece of yarn, return to the circle telling how the Kapok Tree is important to his or her animal. This forms a web of dependence. Once all the animals have joined the web, the teacher will "cut down the tree" to signify deforestation. Discuss how this harms the rainforest's ecosystem.
- Discuss: How could this situation occur in our own community? For example, what happens when a wetland is filled in to build apartments?

*Thanks to Jodi Vines, graduate student, SUNY New Paltz

MATHEMATICS STUDY STRATEGIES

1. Be the Shape

Objective: Students will review geometric shapes by physically forming the shapes.

Activity:

- Display a variety of geometric shape names.

- Model what you want students to do by placing volunteers at specific points on the floor to create a geometric shape. Tell students to lie down, pointing out that each student is one line that makes the shape.

Figure 7.6 Be the Shape

Illustration by Bruce Wasserman

- Place four students in each group and give each group a card naming a shape. Allow groups enough time to plan how to make their shapes. Groups may "borrow" students from another group, if needed.
- Seat the class in a large circle. One at time, each group comes to the center of the circle and forms its shape. Ask students to think of the name of the shape they see. When the teacher counts to three, the students call out the name of the shape in unison, or have students write the name on individual white boards. The teacher then asks for the definition of that shape.

Variation:

- Teacher has cut out geometric shapes on display and points to one. Have students say the name of the shape, and tell how many sides the shape has. Select that number of volunteers to lie on the ground to form that shape. Have the rest of the class say the name of the shape once it has been formed.

- Take a digital photo of the formed shapes and display each student-created geometric shape on a piece of blank poster board or bulletin board.

*Thanks to Melissa Rogers, graduate student, SUNY New Paltz

2. Sharing Cookies

Objective: Students will use cookies to demonstrate their knowledge of division by creating story problems and acting them out for the class to solve.

Activity:

- Begin by reviewing a story problem that was solved by using division.
- Provide cookies that will be used to solve story problems. (Either baked by the class, using other aspects of math in the process, or teacher purchased cookies.) The cookies will be eaten after the activity is completed. Make sure the students all wash their hands before beginning. What a sweet way to deal with math! Yum! Yum!
- Form groups of four students each writing a division story problem using the cookies. Each group will have up to twenty-four cookies to use as they develop their story problem.
- Each group will brainstorm possible scenarios using division. Then they choose one scenario to develop. Plan how it will be acted out, using every member of the group, then practice. When ready (no more than fifteen minutes), each group will present its story problem, and the rest of the class will try to figure out how to solve it.
- After each group presents its division problem, direct them to write the mathematical equation on the chalkboard so the class will see the visual representation of the problem and its solution.
- When all the groups have presented, the class will celebrate their learning by eating their cookies.

Variation:

Create story problems that involve "leftovers/remainders" as a challenge. This can be a great lead in to fraction usage.

For example, four friends want to share ten cookies equally. How can they do this without giving or throwing away any cookies?

Begin with the idea that each friend will get two whole cookies and they must manipulate the remaining two cookies in order to split them up evenly. Therefore, the cookies must be divided in half. When the students can actually divide a cookie in half instead of trying to conceptually visualize it, the learning is more concrete and understandable.

*Thanks to Lilah Weiss, graduate student, SUNY New Paltz

3. Walking Integers

Objective: Students will *feel* an understanding of adding and subtracting integers while acquiring a strategy to assist during tests.
Activity:

- Place a masking tape line on your classroom floor. Mark zero in the center of the line. Use a permanent marker on the masking tape to label positive and negative numbers from 1 to 10. Be sure to space the numbers evenly. Use two different color markers, one for positive numbers and one for negative numbers.
- Taking turns, each student steps on the line at zero, facing the positive numbers. Teacher presents a problem, such as 5 + (–8) = ___. The student walks forward 5 steps (numbers), and then walks back 8 steps (numbers) to arrive at –3, the answer. The stepping movement enables students to *feel* how positive and negative numbers work.
- Do the same with a masking tape strip on each student's desk. This time, tell students to "let their fingers do the walking."
  Example problem: 3 - (–9) = ___.
  Put index finger on zero. Student "finger walks" forward 3 numbers in the positive direction, and then "finger walks" backward 9 numbers in the negative direction to arrive at –6, the answer.
- Show students how they can quickly draw a number line on scrap paper to "finger walk" problems during a test.

4. Finger Multiplication

Objective: Students will use their fingers to memorize the nine times table.
Activity:

- This activity has been around for some time; however, it may be new to some.
- Hold your hands together in front of you so all ten fingers are out in front of you. Number your fingers from one to ten, moving from left to right. The pinky on the left hand is one, the ring finger is two, the left thumb is five, and the right thumb is six. Keep going up to ten, which is the right pinky.
- Select a number you want to multiply by nine, such as three. Fold down your third finger (the middle finger on your left hand). Look at your hands. See how there are two fingers up, then one down, then seven more up. Every finger left of the folded down finger is a ten; every finger right of the folded down finger is a one. So you have two tens and seven ones. This reads as 3 times 9 is 27.
- You can find additional tips for finger multiplication for the 6, 7, and 8 times tables at the following Web site: http://mathforum.org/library/drmath/view/59085.html.

Have fun "fingering" your way to successful test taking.

STUDY STRATEGIES FOR ALL CONTENT AREAS

1. Fallen Word Walls

Objective: Students will walk on word wall words placed on the floor, reading them aloud and stating definitions as they step on each word.
Activity:

- Print vocabulary words (or concepts) students need to learn in any content area on construction paper cards, cut to look like stones or bricks on a path.
- Laminate the cards so they will be reusable and durable. Students can sort the cards into different categories:
  - each content area
  - reading words
    - –structural analysis
    - –phonic patterns
    - –by meaning
- Students walk on words and give definitions for each word. They can also buddy walk, by having one person say the word and having partners give the definition. This is a great way to review before a test!

Variation:

Create a Twister game format. Use either a Twister game mat or make your own using a flannel-backed table cloth, with six rows of circles drawn using four different color permanent markers. Place construction paper circles on the mat's circles, with words to be reviewed. Make a spinner with four boxes: left hand, left foot, right hand, right foot, with each box divided equally into the four colors of the circles on the game mat.

To play: Three to six students stand around the game mat with their shoes off. Someone spins the spinner and calls out what the spinner landed on, such as, "Right hand green." Now the first player puts his right hand on a green circle and says the word on the circle and gives the definition. Repeat this process with each player. On the next round, the first player spins again and the spinner indicates "Left foot yellow." The player must keep his right hand on the green circle while placing his left foot on a yellow circle and reading/defining the word in that circle. Each circle can be used by only one player. Players are eliminated when they fall or when they can't read/define the word. This is an easy to prepare, valuable learning center activity. Upper-grade students can use this game with study groups. It encourages students to study so they can play well.

2. Episodic Memory

Objective: Students will remember a place and recall what was learned there.

Activity:

- Move students to different places in the classroom as new concepts are presented.
  We remember what we learn, *where* we learn it, and the *circumstances* surrounding the learning.
- Visualize where you were when the learning took place to trigger recall.
- Before applying this strategy to academic learning, provide time for students to recall a fact they remember by relating it to the place they learned it. Then share these experiences.

3. Human Continuum

Objective: Students review concepts by moving their bodies on a continuum to show what they are thinking.

Activity:

- Place a line on the floor with masking tape. Place arrows on both ends so it resembles a continuum. Place a large "A" for "agree on one side of the line and a large "D" for "disagree" on the other side. Place a perpendicular piece of tape at the mid-point of the line to represent "I don't know" or "I'm not comfortable sharing what I know."
  The line must be long enough to accommodate all students.
- Students need to bring their notes and anything else they need to bolster their opinions and responses to questions the teacher poses.
- To begin, make a statement about something the students have been studying. Then ask students to move their bodies' locations along the continuum to indicate they agree or disagree with the statement. If they only sort of agree with something, they can move just a little along the line toward the "A," not all the way. The same is true for "disagree." If they don't understand, are confused, or are not comfortable responding, those students should stand at the midpoint of the continuum (at the perpendicular line).
- Here's an example: Say, "All trapezoids are quadrilaterals." Students consider key points—"all," "trapezoid," "quadrilateral"—and then move. Give them up to thirty seconds to get into position.
- After each statement and the students' repositioning, call on several students at different locations to justify their positions with points and counterpoints. Ask those who only partially "agree" or "disagree" to explain their hesitation or to tell what it would take to move them fully one way or the other.
- In the next step, ask students to adjust their positions after hearing their classmates' reasoning. The human continuum can be done at

any point in the lesson: as a preassessment, it is a body kinesthetic anticipation guide or a way to prime the mind. As a midunit check of comprehension, it will point out students who need reteaching. And of course, it's an excellent end-of-unit assessment, since students are getting up, moving, arguing, justifying, and reviewing (Wormeli, 2005).

"My learners move their minds as they move their bodies."

—Mark Reardon

SUMMARY OF KEY CONCEPTS IN THIS CHAPTER

- Body/Kinesthetic Benefits
- Language Arts Study Strategies
  - Act the Word
  - Punctuation: Sounds and Actions
  - Feel the Vowel Spelling
  - Get Physical with Spelling
  - Walking the Review Path
  - Do It with Dance
  - A Friendly Letter
- Social Studies Study Strategies
  - Body Geography
  - Latitude and Longitude Grid
  - Egyptian Social Pyramid
  - Land Form Charades
- Science Study Strategies:
  - Ecosystems
- Mathematics Study Strategies
  - Be the Shape
  - Sharing Cookies
  - Walking Integers
  - Finger Multiplication
- Study Strategies for All Content Areas
  - Fallen Word Walls
  - Episodic Memory
  - Human Continuum

8

Seeing Your Thoughts

Sightseeing on the Visual/Spatial Route

You've heard it said, "A picture's worth a thousand words." Here's why. Pat Wolfe (2001) has stated that the capacity of long-term memory for pictures is unlimited. As a matter of fact, she believes that "a picture is worth at least 10,000 words" (p. 152). Inflation hits the brain! It's why we often hear people say, "I know that person—I just can't remember her name."

As teachers, we need to include visual images as part of our verbal presentations. Those of us who grew up in the era of radio remember sitting next to the radio, intently listening, hearts racing at exciting moments. Remember the Shadow (Lamont Cranston)? "Who knows what evil lurks in the hearts and minds of men?" Our memories hold the excitement of those moments. Clearly, we saw all the action in our minds' eyes.

Today, few students visualize when they read because television, videos, and movies provide all of the images for them. When reading aloud to students, we'd stop after a colorful or action-packed passage to ask, "What do you see?" Usually, only one or two students would raise their hands to share—the avid readers. Then we would prompt the students to "listen carefully to the beautiful language and picture the action" as we reread the passage. Sometimes we'd need to "prime the pump" by doing a "think aloud," sharing and acting out the events in the passage, hoping more students would see the pictures created as the story progressed.

How many of you are incensed when you see a movie of a well-loved book that portrays characters and settings completely different from how you had pictured them? It happened to our students after they had experienced Brian's struggle for survival in Gary Paulsen's book *Hatchet*. Students strongly objected to the way the movie portrayed Brian, as their own understanding of him was so different.

We have learned that students today need assistance building mental pictures of characters and settings when reading. In fact, 87 percent of our learners need visuals (Tileston, 2004). These images increase understanding and transfer information into long-term memory. Maryann Manning (2002), in *Teaching K–8*, stated, "Numerous factors hinder the development of visualization. A lack of background knowledge, inattention to punctuation and phrasing and little personal involvement with the text are three that are significant" (May, 2002).

Teachers can prepare students to visualize by activating prior knowledge. Manning tells us one cannot build a mental picture of an event or situation without prior familiarity or understanding. Discussions before, during and after reading or lecture stimulate personal connections that hook into new material and send it down the open highway to long-term memory. Ask students the following questions:

- "What did you see when ____?"
- "Why do you think you formed that image?"

Or do a think-aloud:

- "When I read (or heard) _____, I immediately pictured (give great detail)."
- "What did you see?"

When studying, it's these pictures that enable us to remember! Enhance instruction with visual images:

- Put basic diagrams on the board as concepts or directions are explained; use stick figures, lines, and arrows to aid understanding.
- List key words as you speak.
- Use pictures and charts.
- Use different colors to delineate each new concept.
- Make sure the image is concrete—preferably, a noun.
- Present positive images to make them memorable.

ACE VISUALIZATION

To become an **ACE** at visualization, Pat Wolfe suggests using the following strategy:

> **A**—Action
> **C**—Color
> **E**—Exaggeration

To assist in remembering anything, create a picture of it in your mind. To make that picture easily retrievable, give it lots of action and use colors to make it vivid and unforgettable. Exaggerate features, possibly making them ridiculous and bizarre, insuring strong connections. The humor of the picture assists in quick recall. Students can be taught to be ACE visualizers.

"There are two types of visual learners—picture and print. Although very different types of learners, they are usually lumped into one category. The result is that picture learners are often mistakenly given printed-language techniques instead of pictures to help them learn" (Willis & Hodson, 1999, p. 147). Visual material for picture learners includes charts, graphs, maps, drawings, movies, and graphic organizers. "Print learners benefit from marking the material as they read it (e.g., underlining or using a highlighter), taking notes in a word-mapping (information mapping using words and no pictures) or outline format, writing down incoming auditory information, and translating visual information into words" (Willis & Hodson, 1999, p. 149). Keeping this in mind, help students pick and choose which of the following activities work best for them.

LANGUAGE ARTS STUDY STRATEGIES

1. Guided Visual Practice for Active Listening

Objective: Students will draw and caption four pictures to identify targeted information, such as main idea, conflict, and theme or lesson.
Activity:
   Teacher will present a read-aloud, two times.

1. Before the first reading, have students set a purpose for listening: main idea, important details, setting, characters, conflict, theme or moral, etc.
2. Do the first reading; it's easier to begin with a short fiction story or folk tale.
3. Before the second reading, ask students to fold a piece of paper into four equal boxes and number them. Read the same material a second time, stopping at four (or fewer) predetermined places.
4. At each breakpoint, direct students to sketch a quick picture showing important events in that section. Allow one to two minutes. Stick figures are fine!
5. After the story or article is finished and pictures are completed, have students go back and write a caption or sentence below the picture, summarizing what happened in each section.
6. Discuss what was drawn and written in each box.
7. On the back of the paper, have students write a title for the story.
8. Below the title, instruct students to write the theme.
9. Discuss titles and themes and why they were chosen.

To carry this activity to higher levels of thinking, repeat this process with a related informational article. Adapt from a text you use or write your own piece if you can't find something appropriate. Now challenge students to find relationships between the texts.

(Thanks to Cinthia Goepfrich, Carmel Central School District)

The Two Frogs is a suitable folktale for this strategy.

The Two Frogs
By Pete Seeger

There were once two frogs. One was a so-be-it frog. It always said, "That's the way things are. We can't change them." The second was a why-is-it frog. It always said, "Why are things this way? Can't we change them?"

The two frogs lived in a pond near a big dairy farm. And one evening, they were hopping along when they came across a tall can of milk with its cover left off. Earlier, the farmer had sold some of the milk to his neighbors, but he had forgotten to cover the milk and store it away for safekeeping.

Back in those days, farmers kept their milk in tall, forty-eight-quart cans, which were called "hundred weights." Usually a farmer had a cold spring with a little house around it—a springhouse—where he stored the milk overnight. The cool water kept the milk fresh until morning when it could be trucked off to the creamery.

———————————————Break point———————————————

"I wonder what's in that can?" said the so-be-it frog.

"Yes, I wonder, too?" said the why-is-it frog. They were both curious.

Well, the two frogs hopped into the can. **S-p-l-a-s-h!** went the so-be-it frog. **S-p-l-a-s-h!** went the why-is-it frog. But because the tall can was only half full, the two frogs soon discovered that they couldn't hop out. Nighttime was fast approaching. The farmer was going to bed. And after thrashing around a bit, the two frogs were both about to drown.

———————————————Break point———————————————

The so-be-it frog said, "There's no hope." And with one last gurgle, he sank to the bottom.

The why-is-it grog said, "Hey, wait! Are you sure there's no hope? There must be some other way."

The why-is-it frog kept on splashing…

And splashing and kicking…

And kicking and splashing.

———————————————Break point———————————————

In the morning, the farmer woke up and said, "Uh-oh! I left that half can of milk out last night." And he ran out to the barn without even bothering to change out of his pajamas.

And what do you think he found?

One tired but very alive frog sitting on top of a big cake of butter.

See an example of visuals and captions in Figure 8.1.

Figure 8.1 Guided Visual Practice for Active Listening

A sample title given on the back could be, "Two Curious Frogs," or a main idea sentence such as "Frog's kicking keeps him alive."

A sample theme on the back could be "It pays to keep trying," "Never give up," or "There's always hope."

SOCIAL STUDIES STUDY STRATEGIES

1. Spacing Sparks A-HA Moments

Objective: Students will see meaning relationships and connections by spacing information logically rather than in straight paragraph form.
Activity:

1. Students need to memorize the Preamble to the U.S. Constitution for example, or any other material.

2. Spacing material into patterns enables students to visualize and note the key words in each section.
   We the people of the United States, in order to form a more perfect Union,
   establish justice,
   insure domestic tranquility,
   provide for the common defense,
   promote the general welfare,
   and **secure** the blessings of liberty
   to ourselves and our posterity,
   do **ordain** and **establish** this Constitution of the United States of America.

Presented in this format, guide students to notice the following:
   - The Preamble is only one sentence long.
   - The words establish, insure, provide, promote, secure, and ordain are all verbs and tell "why" the people need to form a more perfect union.
   - The first seven words tell "who."
   - The last phrase tells "what" will be done.
   - This structure enables students to see the first letter of each verb— *e, i, p, p, s*—which are easily remembered using a mnemonic.
   - finally, add actions or sing it (see "Schoolhouse Rock").

3. Just retyping with meaningful spacing provides a framework to analyze patterns, enables the mind to grasp concepts, and readily marches information into long-term memory. For many, this becomes an **"AHA"** moment!

2. Forms of Government Graphic

Objective: Students will learn the three branches of government and what each does, using the format provided.
Activity:

1. Present the structure of the United States government in key words, using the matrix format.

BRANCH	WHO	WHAT
Legisla**tive**	Senate (2) House of Representatives (by population)	Makes *laws*
Execu**tive**	President Vice President Cabinet	Carries out the *laws*
Judicial **(judge)**	Supreme Court & lower courts	Interprets meaning and applies *laws*

2. Each student makes a copy of this chart.

3. Assist students in seeing that column one names each government branch, column two describes people in the branch of government (WHO), and column three tells how each branch of the government deals with laws (WHAT they do).

4. Recite the information moving from left to right, branch by branch. Repeat frequently.

5. Begin covering the boxes as material is learned, until eventually, all boxes are covered and students picture the matrix chart in their minds and can recite the information.

3. Maps to Memory

Objective: Students will label blank maps, including correct country names and physical features, from memory.
Activity:

1. Teacher prepares outline maps (see example map of Africa in appendix) by noting locations to be learned using
   –numbers for countries.
   –capital letters for geographic features.

2. Students are given a list of locations and features to be learned with correct spellings and the blank map with letters and numbers. Using an atlas or textbook as a reference, students label the given locations on the map. Students need to write out the entire location names, no abbreviations.

3. The class checks the information together and teacher checks accuracy of each student's map. This is the students "master copy map."

4. Students label a second blank map without looking at the first to see how many correct locations they can recall. They then check this map against their master copy map and fill in any items omitted.

Comparing is a key thinking skill and helps to move information into long-term memory.

5. Students label a third blank map to see how many more places they can now label correctly. Students again compare their work to their "master copy map" for correctness. Class shares hints and strategies they used to help make the correct name-location connections.

Sharing of these study tricks is powerful. It helps students make connections, builds self-esteem in the students who share, and provides study hints the teacher can share with other classes.

6. Repeat Step 5.

7. Students work together in teams of two, three, or four to see which team can most quickly label the maps without looking at the master copy. Teammates need to assist team members who are struggling.

Gentle competition and cooperative learning motivates students to continue studying.

8. Students work with a partner to again quickly and correctly label their maps. This time they are challenged to see how quickly the entire class can correctly complete the task. Each time this is done, they try to reduce the class time needed to label their maps.

Steps 5, 7, or 8 may be repeated as often as needed. Lynn's students refer to this activity as "map races."
(With thanks to Lynn Kenny, Arlington High School, Arlington Central Schools, Arlington, NY)

Alternative:
Regional U.S.A.

1. Present a political map of the United States.

Figure 8.3 Small U.S. outline map

2. Moving from east to west, section the states from north to south as follows:
   –states touching the Atlantic Ocean
   –Great Lake states and southern states east of the Mississippi River
   –central states
   –Rocky Mountain states
   –states touching the Pacific Ocean, including Alaska and Hawaii

3. Using the procedure given, practice filling in the U.S. map region by region so that students will be able to picture the U.S. in their "minds' eye." In addition, recite the states by region, in unison, again and again.

4. Share hints and strategies used in learning, such as the following, many of which were developed by students:
   –*V*ermont is shaped like a *V*.
   –*M*assachusetts is a *m*uscleman, flexing his bicep for Cape Cod.
   –*M*ichigan is shaped like a *m*itten.
   –Kentucky is shaped like a drumstick from Kentucky Fried Chicken. Hokey, but it works!
   –*L*ouisiana is shaped like an *L*. Remember that Baton Rouge is the capital by visualizing "Anna" with rosy, *rouge* cheeks, twirling her *baton*.
   –Oklahoma is shaped like a meat cleaver, chopping down on Texas—both produce beef cattle.
   –The southwest border of Montana looks like the outline of "Helena's" face, drooling down on Idaho's baked potato.
   –Don't forget to develop a trick for the four corners' states with your students.

SCIENCE STUDY STRATEGIES

1. Three-Dimensional Visuals

Objective: Students will create three-dimensional models of webs and outlines to organize facts.
Activity:

1. Students can organize information through outlines or through webbing. Topics that are linear, with some order or sequence, lend themselves to outlines. Topics that are open-ended and flexible are comfortably webbed. Webs may have complex information and may branch off in many different directions. Have students determine which organizational format is best for their learning style and for the content.

2. Begin by showing both a traditional outline and web. Next, demonstrate a three-dimensional model of each, to help students better understand them. For the three-dimensional outline, pick a simple topic from a text and place large and small marshmallows on a wet, wooden skewer to represent the outline pattern. Different size beads can also be strung to create an outline format.

Figure 8.4 Three-Dimensional Visuals

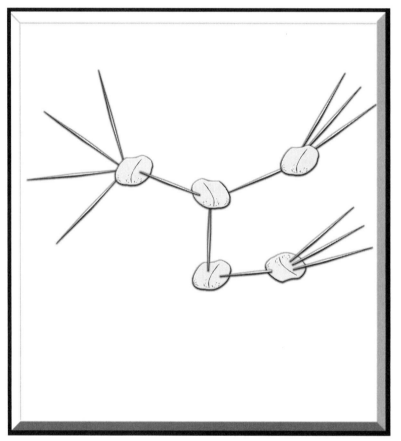

Illustration by Bruce Wasserman

3. Toothpicks and small gumdrops can create the different sections of a web. Use different color gumdrops for each cluster on the web, to visually distinguish between each category.

4. Both webs and outlines make excellent visual organizational and study tools.

(Adapted from *The Organized Student: Teaching Time Management* [Vurnakes, 1995].)

MATHEMATICS STUDY STRATEGIES

1. Measurement Tree

Objective: Students will create a representation to visually compare the cups, pints, and quarts in a gallon.

Figure 8.5 Measurement Tree

Illustration by Bruce Wasserman

Activity:

1. Discuss the components of a gallon:
   2 cups = 1 pint
   2 pints = 1 quart
   4 quarts = 1 gallon

2. Have students draw the trunk of a tree and label it "gallon."

3. Next, add four branches, each labeled "quart."

4. Each branch will sprout two leaves, labeled "pint."

5. Finally, each leaf will have two apples, labeled "cup."

6. The resultant gallon tree is a unique study tool, so that students will no longer ask, "How many cups are in a quart?" which is a commonly asked question in all grades!

(With thanks to Arlington Central School teachers, Arlington, NY)

Alternatives:

- Design a tree to represent the components of a yard
- Draw a tree to represent the parts of a dollar
- Construct a tree to demonstrate metric units

STUDY STRATEGIES FOR ALL CONTENT AREAS

1. Bingo Board

Objective: Students will study vocabulary in any content area by making a Bingo board and playing the game.

Activity:

1. Provide each student with a blank Bingo sheet (see Appendix). Instruct students to write one vocabulary word in each box. Allow them to select one box as a free space.

2. Play Bingo with the teacher calling the word meanings. Players cover their word choice with a small square of paper or a chip. When a player covers a row of boxes, he or she calls out "BINGO!" To be a winner, the player needs to say the word covered and give its meaning or explain it.

3. Bingo follow-up: As homework, *picture learners* will draw a picture to explain the word meaning on the back of each square. *Print learners* will write just *one key word* on the back of the card as a clue to its meaning. In class the next day, students share their pictures or key words with a partner. Now play Bingo using pictures or key words. Once again, the teacher calls the word meanings or uses a cloze technique, filling in the blank with the vocabulary word.

4. Students may now cut the boxes apart to make "instant" flash cards.

5. Suggestions for flash card use:
   - Go through the flash cards, making two piles: words that are "confidently known" and words that still need to be studied.
   - Review the words that still need to be studied.
   - As words are learned, those cards may go into the "confidently known" pile.
   - If after three or four repetitions, the words are not learned, the student needs to *use other alternatives or strategies* to learn them. See more ideas in this book!
   - Before the test, put both piles of cards together and do a final review of all words.

2. Picture Relay

Objective: Students will review vocabulary words in any content area by drawing a picture that represents the word so teammates can guess the correct word.

Activity:

1. Divide the class into two or more teams. Player one from each team goes to the chalkboard or whiteboard. The teacher privately shows each player the vocabulary word. Players are given "think time." When the teacher says, "Go!" the drawing players walk to the board and draw a picture to represent the word while their teammates watch. It's fine to use stick figures. The first team to correctly guess the word gets a point. The game continues until all the vocabulary words have been reviewed. This acts as a good incentive for students to study.

Alternatives:

For more active participation, each student writes an answer and one point is given for every correct answer.

3. Creative Vocabulary Poster

Objective: Students will facilitate in-depth learning of vocabulary words by creating posters.

Activity:

1. Assign one vocabulary word per student, or have each student select a word that is difficult.

2. The poster vocabulary word needs to be spelled correctly and printed in lettering that helps create the meaning—that is, concrete poetry style.

Figure 8.6 Creative Vocabulary Poster

Illustration by Bruce Wasserman

3. Select a dictionary definition, based on context. Students write the definition in their own words (not copied directly from the dictionary).

4. Write an antonym for the word.

5. Let pictures convey the meaning. Use stick figures, a drawing, magazine pictures, Clip Art, and so forth.

6. Create conversations in an appropriate setting, using a synonym that shows understanding of the word. Dialogue bubbles or a play-like script may be used. Or, at another level, use the word correctly in an original sentence.

7. Use abundant color—this is where the student can become an ACE visualizer, using Action, Color, and Exaggeration.

8. Optional: Think of an action that conveys the meaning and use movement to demonstrate understanding.

9. Share with the class.

**When a student has been reviewing words
or concepts for a test in any content area,
and "just can't seem to remember,"
do a quick poster draft.
This process may spark a memory link.**

4. Flap Organizers

Objective: Students will create flap organizers to use as study tools in any content.

Activity:

1. Determine items to be studied (from text, board, study sheet, etc.).

2. Fold a piece of paper in half horizontally.

3. Cut the top piece of folded paper to the fold, making as many equal-sized flaps as needed.

4. Write each item to be studied on the front flaps.

5. On the inside top of the flap, write the definition.

6. On the inside bottom, draw a picture to illustrate the definition.

7. On the back, write a title for the flap organizer.

Figure 8.7 Flap Organizer

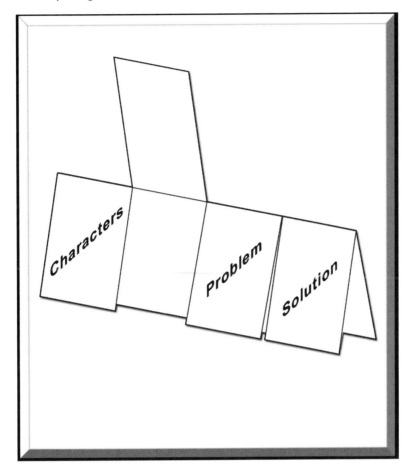

Illustration by Bruce Wasserman

5. Artifact Box

Objective: Students will collect artifacts providing memory pegs for key information learned in a unit and place them in an appropriately designed container.

Activity:

1. The items placed in this container provide memory prompts for review. Teacher will determine the appropriate number of artifacts to be included.

2. Direct students to collect and/or make a variety of items, such as maps, photos, quotes, audiotapes, drawings, and actual items that represent key concepts.

3. Select or make a container appropriate for the theme to house the artifacts. Ideally, this will also act as a review prompt.

4. As students share the contents of their artifact boxes, it acts as review for the entire class.

Variation:

Teacher can create and share an artifact box with the class before beginning a unit to pique interest, like "coming attractions."

GRAPHIC ORGANIZERS

Graphic organizers are visuals that enable us to use both sides of the brain. They allow us to see the parts and the whole simultaneously, which leads to seeing connections and relationships that might not otherwise be evident. Below is a page of graphic organizers from Robin Fogarty and Judy Stoehr (1995) in *Integrating Curricula with Multiple Intelligences*. They lend themselves to a myriad of applications across the curriculum. Some are familiar, and others are unique. Variety excites students! When preparing for a test, challenge students to select a graphic or create their own to organize information. It prompts them to analyze what they are studying and think about it in a new way. See examples in Figure 8.8.

Figure 8.8 Graphic Organizers

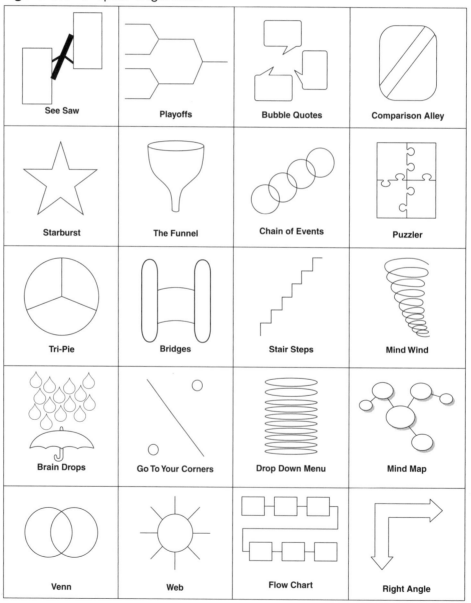

Figure 8.8 Used with permission, Robin Fogarty, Sage Publications and Corwin Press

Figure 8.9 shows applications for several of Fogarty's graphic organizers. Use them to spark your own adaptations.

Figure 8.9 Graphic Organizers

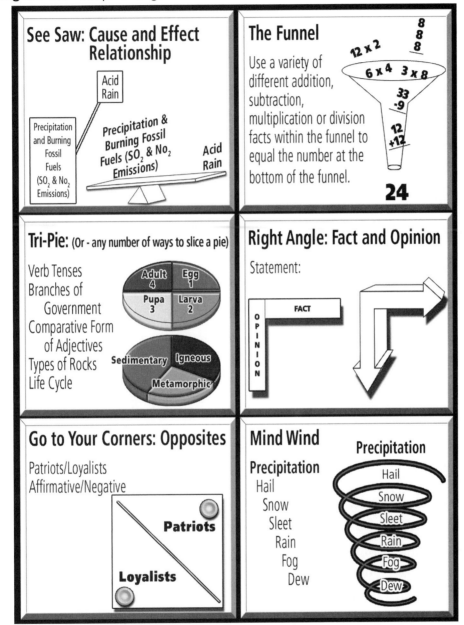

Illustration by Bruce Wasserman

Sports trainers, athletes, dancers visualize their goals.
Test-takers visualize to maximize recall.
EVERYBODY can visualize success!

We include a portion of the following poem because it so perfectly and powerfully sums up the value of imaging. Repeated unison reading of *"What You Can See You Can Be!"* will firmly embed the concept.

What You Can See You Can Be!
by David A. Anderson

You can fight a fire
 If you so desire

Or do a dance
 If you take the chance

Or build a jet
 And learn to fly,
Or whatever you see
 In your mind's eye

Because what you can see,
 YOU CAN BE!

Believe it's so
 And it's true!
It's just that easy;
 It's up to you!

Plant a seed
 Within your mind
And it will blossom
 In due time

Because what you can see,
 CAN BE !

It's very simple;
 Here's what to do
(Now think of something good
 Because it will come true!)
Picture yourself
 Having or being or doing
Whatever you desire today.

Put the picture in a bubble,
 Then let it float away.

Trust that it will happen
 Let go of it all the way;
Don't forget to say thank you,
 Then go outside and play!

Now don't you doubt
 And don't you fear
'Cause that blocks out
 What you want to hear.

Just see it and believe it,
 And claim it's already yours;
Know that it will happen,
 And *that* opens all the doors!

Remember, what you can see,
YOU CAN BE!

The entire poem can be found in David A. Anderson's (1988) book, *What You Can See You Can Be!*

Give students silent time to visualize mental pictures in their "minds' eye" of goals that they want to achieve. Bear in mind that some individuals will close their eyes to visualize, while others are more comfortable with their eyes open.

SUMMARY OF KEY CONCEPTS IN THIS CHAPTER

- Power of Visuals
- ACE Visualization Technique
- Language Arts Study Strategies
    - Guided Visual Practice for Active Listening
    - "The Two Frogs" Folktale
- Social Studies Study Strategies
    - Spacing Sparks A-HA Moments
    - Forms of Government Graphic
    - Maps to Memory
- Science Study Strategies
    - Three-Dimensional Visuals
- Math Study Strategies
    - Measurement Tree
- Study Strategies for All Content Areas
    - Bingo Board
    - Picture Relay
    - Creative Vocabulary Poster
    - Flap Organizers
    - Artifact Box
- Graphic Organizers
- What You Can See You Can Be!

9

Organizing to Know

Marching Down Trails of Logic

"My brain's a meaning seeking
pattern making,
purpose detecting
organ of the mind."

—Reardon

"It can learn isolated facts, but it will recall them better with themes, the larger related picture, and interdisciplinary relationships. The best content is both fact-related and thematic. It's related to other learning, disciplines, and our own lives" (Redenbach, 2003, p. 97). Logically strong learners look for patterns, relationships, formulas, and chunking when connecting new learning into long-term memory. They approach tasks methodically, organizing and analyzing materials and information. Making comparisons, seeing things in sequence, and thinking concretely all assist efficient study habits.

We can help build logic strength by teaching students to organize using matrices as well as categorizing information. Additionally, developing maps, flowcharts, or time lines are useful organizational systems for learners traveling this trail. Teachers need to provide these structures for students who do not innately see them.

CHUNKING INFORMATION

Pat Wolfe (2001) explained chunking as any meaningful unit of information grouped together in a class or category. A word is a chunk of letters, remembered as easily as a single letter (but carrying much more information). Being able to see how information fits together in chunks is, therefore, a hallmark of learning, a way of working with larger and larger amounts of information. For instance, we easily remember our social security numbers as three chunks of information, not as nine separate digits. Feden and Vogel (2003) explained that chunking allows more information to be held in our working memory—if pieces "become chunks, then working memory can hold five to nine chunks of information, greatly increasing the amount of information that can be held, and manipulated, in working memory to work on cognitive tasks" (Connell, 2005, p. 107).

Wolfe (2001) noted, "The difference between novices and experts in a field appears to be that experts tend—because of a great deal of experience in a field—to organize information into much larger chunks, while novices work with isolated bits of information" (p. 100). Think about expert football players and how many plays they have stored in their long-term memories. The same is true of experts in any other area—musicians, athletes, scientists, chefs, lawyers, and especially **expert teachers!**

Complex subjects or long strings of information will be remembered when it is chunked into segments. Think of numbers that we easily remember because they are chunked into groups of two to four numbers: phone numbers, social security numbers, zip codes, and even credit card numbers! The human brain can remember five to seven chunks of information at one time, but this varies depending on both prior learning and the learner's age. There should be no more than seven chunks and preferably only three to five. Chunking data improves recall.

Take thirty to forty-five seconds to memorize the following list:

149217761812192919632000

When the time is up, cover the list. Now, write down all the numbers you remember—there are twenty-four! Was it difficult? Not if you're a "chunker"! Now look at these numbers and find meaningful units. Again, look for thirty to forty-five seconds, cover the list, and write down as many numbers as you now remember.

Let's try it again with letters:

NASACBSTVDARCIAACLU

After thirty to forty-five seconds, cover the letters and write down as many as you recall. If you looked for meaningful chunks, recall would have been easier this time.

Turn to the next page to check your answers and discover how meaningful chunks simplify memory.

Of course, there is no right or wrong way to chunk information—the key point is that students need to make the chunking connections themselves, and then the chunking has meaning to each learner.

"In fact, visual chunking is the most effective way to remember information. This is why webbing and concept maps are effective teaching tools. They help students see how information is related, helping them chunk it and connect it to information they already have (Connell, 2005, p. 107)."

PATTERNS—MORE IMPORTANT THAN FACTS

The human brain is naturally motivated to see and use patterns, but students' abilities to pattern depends on their background knowledge. Brain theorist Leslie Hart (1983) reminded us that "pattern recognition depends heavily on what experience one brings to a situation" (p. 67). Students need to organize information, then revise and change it as new information is added, plus pass it through the filters of their own experiences. "Learning is the extraction of meaningful patterns from confusion" (Jensen, 1995, p. 17).

Where do we find patterns—Plants, food groups, musical themes, numbers, chapter headings in a book, learning styles, cells in a body, types of behaviors, and so forth. **PATTERNS ARE EVERYWHERE!** When students can see structural patterns, they will learn the value of organizing ideas as they read and study, and they will not be frustrated by their inabilities to remember. Some students will love pattern seeking; it will torment others.

Try the following examples:

1, 6, 11, 16, 21, ___, ___

a, b, d, e, ___, ___, ___, ___

Chicago, Michigan, Miami, Connecticut, _____, _____

Banana, carrot, lettuce, apple, _____, _____, _____

29, 47, 65, ___, ___

1492 1776 1812 1929 1963 2000
NASA CBS TV DAR CIA ACLU
Pattern: + 5
Pattern: 2 consecutive letters, skip 1 letter
Pattern: city, state
Pattern: 1 fruit, 2 vegetables
Pattern: tens increase by 2 and ones decrease by 2

It's easy to do when you discover significant dates in history for the numbers and meaningful acronyms for the letters.

Now, try solving some "Pundles," written by sixth-grade students (George Fischer Middle School, Carmel, New York, 1993).

1. ban ana

2. comm ercial

3. DIPPER

4. play play

5. fa st

6. T
   O
   U
   C
   H

Practical Ways to Apply Patterning

Logical patterning assists students in everyday learning and studying. As students discover and use the **"AHA"** awareness of patterns, the excitement cements learning. The emotional charge of the **"AHA"** tightens the connection into long-term memory.

Content Specific Patterns

- In language arts, there are short story plot plans, character behavior, sentence patterns, syllable patterns, and poetry such as haiku, cinquain, and AABB.
- In social studies, there are survival needs, climatic factors, and supply and demand.
- In science, there are seasons, water cycle, magnetism, plant growth, nutrient cycle, and structure of the atom.
- In math, there are the inverse operations of addition/subtraction and multiplication/division, geometric patterns, nine times table, and even and odd numbers.
- In music, there are symphony movements, waltzes with three beats to a measure, and refrains/chorus.
- In art, there are shapes, symmetry, and color wheel.
- These are just a few examples. Please add your ideas to the patterns.

Answers: 1. banana split, 2. commercial break, 3. big dipper, 4. double play, 5. breakfast, 6. touchdown

PATTERNING ACTIVITIES FOR ALL CONTENT AREAS

1. Categorizing Game

Objective: Students will review content vocabulary words by categorizing and using logical thinking.

Activity:

1. Here are the game rules:
   a. Spelling doesn't count!
   b. Fold a piece of paper into three columns, using two "hot dog" (vertical) folds.
   c. Number each column on the top (1, 2, 3).
   d. Each word dictated needs to be written into one of the three columns/categories.

2. Teacher will prepare three lists of content vocabulary related to units of study being reviewed, having in mind a topic title for each category; however, any title students can justify may be accepted. At times, include a general knowledge list such as those in Figure 9.1.

3. Teacher randomly dictates words one at a time, mixing them from each category. Be sure that all students have written each word before giving the next one. When students are not sure where to place a word, they may write it on the back for the time being. (If students struggle to categorize a word, it may be possible that they do not understand the term. This is a "heads-up" for the teacher!)

4. After six words (or approximately one third of the words) are given, challenge students to think about *why* they have grouped the words the way they have.

5. Dictate six more randomly selected words (a second third of the words).

6. Now stop. Tell students to reread the words in each list silently and think of a possible title for each list. Encourage students to reread their lists and move words from one list to another to fit these titles better. Then direct them to write the title for each list at the bottom of the column and be prepared to explain their thought process.

7. Dictate the balance of the words. Then direct students to reread their lists to see if any titles need to be changed. At this point, have students move any uncategorized words from the back, to an appropriate column. Challenge students to be sure *every item* in a category fits the title; **rewrite titles if needed.** Commonly, students will find their first titles will need to be broadened or narrowed. *For example, in word list one (Figure 9.1), if milk, cream, gravy, and lemonade are presented first, "foods" is an appropriate title. However, this title will change as soon as turpentine, oil, or bleach is added.*

8. Discuss the titles and items within each column. As students share, note the various titles given, different ways items are categorized and the thought patterns.

9. The ability to categorize provides a variety of links into long-term memory, thereby making retrieval easier and deepening understanding.

Follow-up activities include the following:

Choose a column and write a paragraph, using most or all words in that column. Point out to students the title will help them write a topic sentence with each word in the list providing supporting details. Each column/list can be considered a paragraph organizer.

Figure 9.1

Categorizing Game Word Lists

Rules: Every word I dictate needs to be written in one of your three columns/categories.
Spelling does not count. Spell as correctly as you can or draw a sketch.
Think about "why" you are grouping the words as you write them in a list.

Word List 1

towels	milk	bobcat
badge	cream	elephant
plates	water	wolf
cups	gravy	turtle
bag	turpentine	squirrel
tissue	oil	salamander
	bleach	frog
	lemonade	rabbit
May be made of paper	*Liquids*	*Has four legs*

Word List 2

saunter	evaporate	hypothesis
skip	rainbow	question
sail	boil	prediction
slither	condense	test
fly	freeze	conclusion
drive	flood	observation
Ways to Move	*Related to Water*	*Scientific Method*

Word List 3

plot	proper	synonyms
exposition	plural	homonyms
setting	common	compounds
rising action	singular	antonyms
characters	possessive	contractions
falling action	direct objects	
climax	sentence subjects	
Parts of a Plot Plan	*Related to Nouns*	*Kinds of Words*

Alternative 1:

Rick Wormeli (2005) in *Summarization in Any Subject* suggested that teachers provide students with index cards or Post-It notes that have facts, concepts, or attributes of the categories being reviewed. Then, put students in small groups to arrange the cards, making and naming appropriate categories. As students weigh their decisions about where each card belongs, *the conversations that ensue are as important to the learning experience as the actual card placement.* Have students defend their reasons, orally and often. Encourage them to question the card placement of other group members. The logical explanations will further cement the learning into long-term memory for both the speaker and the listener. If students can't come to agreement, they will have to return to their notes and textbooks to confirm the facts or concepts. It doesn't get much better than that!

Alternative 2

Put all the index cards to be categorized in a bag. Have each student, one at a time, remove a card from the bag and place it on the chalkboard or chart paper in a category in which he or she feels it belongs. Continue having students place individual cards in categories, and again, encourage them to question placements and discuss decisions as well as reference notes/texts for confirmation. The addition of movement is beneficial for all.

2. Compare/Contrast Matrix

Objective: Students will show similarities and differences between two or more people, places, events, concepts, processes, and so forth using a matrix.

Activity:

1. Students will create a matrix targeting attributes, properties, or characteristics of two or more topics/concepts being studied.

2. The topics/concepts/names can be placed across the top of the matrix (horizontal axis). The attributes/characteristics will be placed down the left side (vertical axis). These positions can be reversed. See the following examples.

Generic Compare and Contrast Matrix

	Item 1	Item 2
Attribute		
Attribute		
Attribute		

Factors Influencing the Outcome of the Civil War Matrix

	Industrialization	Transportation	Population	Resources
North				
South				

Using a matrix forces students to express ideas in key words and moves information from lengthy texts to visual graphics. The logical layout enables students to grasp concepts, draw conclusions, and makes relationships pop out at them. Now, studying becomes a snap!

3. Cycle/Sequence Bracelet

Objective: Students will use colored beads to represent the sequence in a cycle that is studied to retell the cycle steps.
Activity:

1. After students have studied a cyclical topic, they will make a beaded bracelet or necklace to deepen understanding.

2. Present a selection of many different colored beads, with a variety of shapes, plus a length of clear jewelry cord or plastic lacing on which to string the beads.

3. Ask students to select beads that represent/symbolize each step in the cycle. Use different colors, styles, and amounts of beads to delineate each step.

4. Lay the beads out in order and string them using the jewelry cord or plastic lacing. Begin and end with a knot. When all beads are strung, knot bracelet or necklace to fit (Optional: knot between each color).

5. Allow students to share their bracelets with several partners, repeatedly providing opportunities to tell the cycle steps and bead symbols. As students touch the beads and retell the steps, they will be preparing for a test! Before you know it, students will have memorized the cycle and will be eager to share their new piece of jewelry with family and friends (adapted from Glock, Wertz, & Meyer, 1999). See sample water cycle bracelet in Figure 9.2.

Alternative:

Adapt this activity to any sequential information such as time lines or steps in a process.

Rosanne Strouth, a middle school psychologist, attended one of our workshops. She adapted this activity to demonstrate a "cycle of feelings." The bracelet helped students identify their feelings and notice changes in their emotions. Note how she used a combination of words and colors to indicate changing feelings (see Figure 9.3).

Figure 9.2 Water Cycle Bracelet

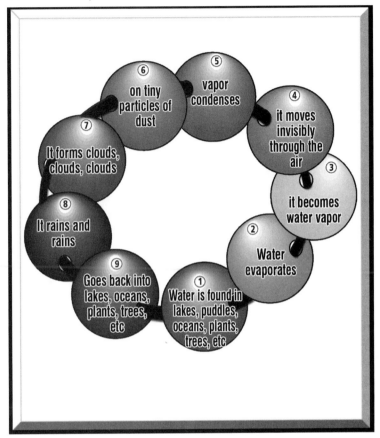

Illustration by Bruce Wasserman

Figure 9.3 Cycle of Feelings

Cycle of Feelings

birth, beginnings,
pure, innocent

rebirth, a new
beginning

happy, fun, good

feeling better,
different, but better

change, different,
no loger fun

heaviness lifting,
new skills, coping

loud noises, voices,
uneasiness, scared

counseling,
someone listens,
understands

fear, sadness,
loneliness

very sad, chronic depression,
feelings of loneliness, anger,
confusion, hopelessness

Credit: Rosanne Strouth. Used with permission.

"The brain is a lean, mean, pattern-making machine."

—Moretz

SUMMARY OF KEY CONCEPTS IN THIS CHAPTER

- The Patterning Brain
- Chunking Information
- Patterns—More Important Than Facts
- Practical Ways to Apply Patterning
    - Content Specific Patterns
- Patterning Activities for All Content Areas
    - Categorizing Game
    - Compare/Contrast Matrix
    - Cycle/Sequence Bracelet

10

Learning Together

It's More Than Just Me

Since the beginning of time, working together has been necessary for survival! In fact, it has been said that the only reason mankind has made it this far in our evolutionary history is our willingness to

- communicate with each other,
- cooperate and collaborate, and
- help each other.

On every front, our postmodern world is rapidly moving from a *me* to a *we* society. In the latter half of the twentieth century, this shift from me to we led us to suggest that the skills of working together and cooperating with each other were instrumental in our progress to this point. They may well be even more important for our survival in the future. To succeed in teamwork, we need to listen attentively, encourage ideas, and praise accomplishments. A brain-positive reason to work in pairs or small groups is that the brain works best with feedback (Lyle, 2006).

Robert Marzano (2001) has identified nine instructional strategies that are most likely to improve student achievement, one of which supports **cooperative learning**. He recommended keeping group sizes small, not overusing the strategy, and varying objectives. Design group work around Johnson and Johnson's (1994) core cooperative learning components: positive interdependence, group processing, appropriate use of social skills, face-to-face interaction, and individual and group accountability.

STUDY GROUPS

Cooperative group work is regularly used for working in the educational community. We form literature circles to read books, small groups to work on social studies or science projects, and jigsaw activities. What we tend to overlook, however, is forming groups and allowing class time for review and study. To optimize learning, keep group size to three or four students. Some of the values of group study are that it

- communicates to students the importance of studying since class time is being provided,
- models a variety of ways to study,
- provides a structured setting to practice and review materials,
- promotes clearing up confusion with difficult concepts,
- enables students to teach their classmates,
- is a win-win for the student who teaches and the student who needs to review,
- motivates repetition,
- makes studying become fun in a relaxed atmosphere, and
- encourages students to study knowing others are counting on them.

The teacher's role in cooperative study groups is to

- provide group time in class,
- check to see that each student has a copy of all the notes and study sheets,
- set specific goals for the group, focusing on small portions of data, expecting every student in the group to master the information (see Marzano, 2001; Johnson & Johnson, 1994),
- provide reasonable time limits—fifteen minutes is enough (If the groups become chatty, they're done!),
- appoint a "task master" in each group to keep everyone focused,
- select "reporters" to communicate how each group studied and to share successful study techniques, and
- celebrate group successes.

Asking students to reflect on discussion/study group work raises retention of information (Reardon, 2006). In doing so, students discover a variety of ways study groups work effectively when given time to think about how they learned—metacognition time.

Early in the school year, provide an opportunity for students to exchange phone numbers and e-mail addresses with three or four classmates—ones they believe will be responsible study partners. These are peers they can contact when they have been absent, need homework clarification, or want to collaborate with a **study buddy**.

Teachers can encourage parents to host study buddy groups. Parent responsibilities include

- providing transportation,
- serving snacks (not sugary) during study breaks (see Chapter 4, Nutrition),
- having necessary supplies available.

To enable students to experience and analyze the cooperative process, we recommend the West African Rock Game (Boggeman, Hoer, & Wallack, 1996). It is a wonderful metaphor for the interdependence of learners in the classroom and promotes active problem solving.

West African Rock Game

1. Each student will need two smooth, round rocks. But begin practicing without using the rocks, to get the rhythm.

2. Have students sit in a circle with legs crossed and knees touching those next to them. While students are in the circle, they chant, "pick up, click, pass, clap" while going through the motions as if they had the rocks. The count is 4/4 and everything happens on the downbeat. After practicing a few times, add the rocks and play the game. Eventually there is no chanting—just actions.

3. Everyone reaches down and picks up two rocks, clicks them together, places them in front of the person to the right, claps once and then starts again. Pick up the rocks on one, click the rocks on two, pass the rocks to the person to the right on three, and clap hands on four. Repeat. Begin slowly at first, counting the cadence aloud. This continues until the rhythm is learned and the movement flows.

4. The rhythm is quite simple. When attempted as a whole, however, it is not easy to maintain the rhythm for any length of time. After many attempts, when the rhythm begins to flow, smiles are everywhere. Encourage the students to look up and watch the choreographic by-product of the game as everyone moves in unison. Inevitably, something will happen to disrupt the even flow of rocks. When the rhythm falls apart, there are ample opportunities for discussion. Asking "Who sped up the tempo?" or "Who slowed it down?" forces the students to consider who is leading and who is following. The truth is no one person can change the tempo of the group. Everyone has a set of rocks. Everyone must go faster or more slowly, or it will not work. A person cannot continue the rhythm until the rocks are passed. The goal is to sound like one big rock clicking and one large set of hands clapping. What happens when a rock is dropped and only one is passed on? Does everyone stop? Is there a way to keep going and correct the problem? Every student is at a different level of ability when it comes to playing and keeping a rhythm. Some will find this easy, while others will need more practice. The group must develop a plan that will allow *everyone* to work as one, despite their different abilities.

It is appropriate at this time to ask students to generate a list of guidelines for teamwork.

Classroom Applications

The brain loves games and students think that when they are playing games, they're not "working." With that in mind, here are some fun ways to actively review with students.

1. Who or What Am I?

Objective: Students will review any content materials by asking questions that can be answered with only "yes" or "no," to identify *who* or *what*.
Activity:

1. Students will each have a sign taped on their backs with a vocabulary word or concept being reviewed.

2. Participants will ask questions that can only be answered with yes or no, in order to determine what sign is taped on their backs.

3. Students will do this as a whole class, mingling and asking questions. As soon as they figure out who or what is on their card, they may circulate and assist others. The game ends when all students have figured out their own words.

Optional: Students take turns sharing the words that were on their backs and giving one to three key words to define the words.

2. Inside-Outside Circles

Objective: Students will write questions and answers to review unit content.
Activity:

1. Prepare for this activity by assigning the following homework the previous night: Write two or three questions and answers that review unit concepts and vocabulary.

   Provide index cards for the questions. Motivate students to write questions by telling them anyone who comes to class without questions will be unable to participate. (They will write their questions while the circles review together.)

2. Form two circles, as equal in number as possible. Have circles face each other and pair up. Begin with members of the outside circle asking their partners on the inside one question. If the answer is incorrect, the questioner provides the correct answer. Switch. Now, the inside person asks the question. Next, direct the outside circle to rotate three people to the right. Repeat the question/answer process. Change which circle rotates, the number of people they rotate, and the direction they rotate, as you wish.

Optional: Collect student questions and inform students that several of their questions will be included on the unit test.

3. Toss-It Review

Objective: Students will review any unit content (spelling words, vocabulary, or math facts work especially well) by catching a beanbag or Nerf ball, then answering questions.

Activity:

1. Students stand in a circle. The teacher asks a question. Allow **think time**, and then throw a beanbag or Nerf ball to a student who answers the question. If the catcher can't answer, he or she can ask up to three people for clues. If still unable to answer, the teacher provides the answer. Then the catcher becomes the next thrower, asking a question, giving think time, and tossing the ball. (Use only underhanded tosses.)

Alternatives:

1. Teacher tosses a beanbag or Nerf ball to a student who tells one important thing learned in the unit. This student then tosses to another student who repeats what the thrower learned and adds one thing she or he learned. That student tosses to another student, who repeats what the second student learned and adds another fact. Continue as time and attention permit.

2. Create a yarn spider web, connecting all students. Students stand in a circle. Teacher begins by asking a question about the content being reviewed and allows think time. Then teacher unravels a bit of yarn, holds the end, and tosses the yarn ball to a student. (Use underhanded tosses only.) The catcher answers, asks another question, allows think time, and then, holding onto the yarn, unravels some, and tosses the yarn ball to another student to answer. Repeat, until everyone has had a turn, which will create a yarn spider web, demonstrating the interconnectedness of the class. The other way this spider web can be created is by having students state one piece of important information learned in the unit of study.

4. Fraction Cubes

Objective: Students will make game cubes and work in groups of three to review fractional math problems, using all operations.

Activity:

1. Hand out one cube template, printed on cover or card stock, for each student. See Appendix for the pattern.

2. Put students in groups of three, and assign each student a number from one to three.
   -Number ones write a different fraction in each of their six cube boxes.
   -Number twos write a different mixed number in each of their six cube boxes.

-Number threes write a subtraction, addition, multiplication, and division sign, then two more signs (their choice from the four operations) in each of their six cube boxes.

3. Have students carefully cut out the templates.

4. Model how to fold the template into a cube. Students fold their own cubes and tape them closed.

5. Let the game begin! Player one will roll all three cubes. A math problem will appear. The mixed number will be the first part of the problem; the sign will tell which operation needs to be used; and the fraction will be the second part of the problem. (The reason for this is that when subtracting, the larger number always needs to go first. To make the directions simpler, have students always put the mixed number first.) Player one will have two minutes to solve the problem on a piece of scrap paper. While player one is solving the problem, the other two players also have jobs to do. One will watch the clock, timing two minutes, and the other will calculate the answer and check for correctness.

6. If player one is correct, he or she gets one point.

7. Player two now rolls the cubes.

8. Play continues until the teacher signals stop. The players with the most points in each group stand while the class gives them a round of applause.

9. Provide sandwich bags to store game cubes. Alternate the groups' cubes and play again another day.

Alternative one: Provide three additional cube templates for each student to make game cubes for continued review at home.

Alternative two: For younger children this can be done with whole numbers—first single digits, and later with tens and hundreds.

Thanks to Joann Gradzki, graduate student at SUNY New Paltz.

"If we don't model what we teach, we are teaching something else."

—A. Maslow

"There is no 'I' in teamwork!"

SUMMARY OF KEY CONCEPTS
IN THIS CHAPTER

- Interpersonal background We, Not Me!
- Study Groups
  - –The Values of Study Groups
- Building Teamwork: West African Rock Game
- Classroom Applications
  - –*Who* or *What* am I?
  - –Inside-Outside Circles
  - –Toss-It Review
  - –Fraction Cubes

11

Timing Is Everything

Planning the Journey

"Time is an equal opportunity, nonrenewable resource."

No matter how important you are, no matter how rich or poor, you get 168 hours to spend each week—no more, no less (Ellis, 1997, p. 39).

How we use our time is determined by what we allow to control it. If we don't manage our responsibilities, they will manage our lives. Let's take a look at two student scenarios.

Sue, a sixth grader, said, "My teachers think school work is all I have to do after school. It's not. I have chores, dance lessons, and clubs, as well as religion class and family activities. AND, what about friends? There's never enough time for everything!"

A teacher was overheard complaining in the faculty room: "I phoned Tom's mother because his science project was due today and he didn't turn it in." His mom's response was, "What project? I had no idea Tom even had a project assignment."

Obviously, Sue's time is not under her control, and Tom seems to have no clue how to manage his time to meet school responsibilities. Both Sue and Tom clearly need time management tips to gain control of their lives. Learning to manage time gives everyone the power to use this most *valuable resource* in the ways they choose.

MANAGING YOUR TIME

The first step is to become conscious of what's happening in your life and when it happens. Use the after school calendar (see Figure 11.1) to slot in weekly personal activities such as sports—both practices and games—, lessons, rehearsals, religious school, TV shows you plan to watch, work, and so forth. Make weekly copies and add other appointments such as medical or social events. When all activities are filled in, chunks of available study time become evident. This calendar helps organize and prioritize your life.

Figure 11.1   Weekly calendar

AFTER SCHOOL CALENDER

TIME	MONDAY	TUESDAY	WEDNESDAY	THURSDAY	FRIDAY	WEEKEND
3:00–3:30						
3:30–4:00						
4:00–4:30						
4:30–5:00						
5:00–5:30						
5:30–6:00						
6:00–6:30						
6:30–7:00						
7:00–7:30						
7:30–8:00						
8:00–8:30						
8:30–9:00						
9:00–9:30						
9:30–10:00						
10:00–10:30						
10:30–11:00						
11:00–11:30						

The next step is to coordinate the after school calendar with the week-at-a-glance homework sheet shown (see Figure 11.2). Teachers need to put homework assignments on the board for students to copy onto this sheet. Until doing this becomes automatic and accurate, we recommend teachers check and initial this homework sheet daily. Additionally, train students to write in "BK," indicating that their textbook is needed, and "no HW" when there is no homework. Be consistent—write homework assignments in the same location daily. Request that parents initial the week-at-a-glance homework sheet when they have seen the completed homework. Note that parents do not have to check the accuracy of the homework; just see that the student work corresponds to the homework assignment. After three to four weeks of daily signing, teachers can cut back to weekly checking of homework sheets.

Figure 11.2 Week-at-a-Glance Homework Sheet

WEEK-AT-A-GLANCE

MONDAY	TUESDAY	WEDNESDAY	THURSDAY	FRIDAY
date:	date:	date:	date:	date:
Math	Math	Math	Math	Math
Science	Science	Science	Science	Science
Social Studies	Social Studies	Social Studies	Social Studies	Social Studies
Language Arts	Language Arts	Language Arts	Language Arts	Language Arts
Reading	Reading	Reading	Reading	Reading
Other:	Other:	Other:	Other:	Other:
Parent Signature:				
Teacher Signature:				

Many schools provide student planners, which have more space for daily assignments and lend themselves to planning long-term projects. One planner source is Premier School Agendas (www.premieragendas.com). Planners are valuable for homework assignments, planning long-term projects, and communications with parents, and they assist with organization, time management, and study strategies.

When presenting long-term projects, model breaking the assignment into manageable increments and recording the intermediate due dates for each part in the planner or on a week-at-a-glance homework sheet. Work backward from the final due date and consider the

- difficulty of the task/materials;
- time needed for each piece; and
- presentation mode such as handwritten notes, typed, visuals, power point, charts, and so forth.

In addition, note when a test is scheduled, and write "study" in the preceding days.

Stress how planning is an adult skill; show adult planners (calendars) and tell how corporations train employees in their use. Today, many adults carry personal digital assistants (PDAs), which are electronic planners and organizers, or Blackberries, and they never leave home without them! Time management is about life skills: setting goals, prioritizing, planning ahead, budgeting time, meeting deadlines, caring for possessions, and taking responsibility. Teachers and parents who teach children time management and organization skills early are giving students a huge advantage in life (Dunnewind, 2003).

WAYS TO MAXIMIZE STUDY AT HOME

Don't wait for inspiration to strike—it probably won't. We can learn a lesson about studying from observing an athlete. Can you imagine seeing an athlete who is training for a mile run sitting on the field waiting for an inspiration to strike before he starts to practice? No way! He trains strenuously day after day whether he wants to or not. Like the athlete, we get in training for our tests and examinations by doing the things we're expected to do over a long period of time (whether we want to or not!) (Bragstad & Stumpf, 1982, p. 307).

Figure 11.3

Strategies to Optimize Study

- Establish a consistent homework time within the constraints of the child's after school calendar. Work done during daylight hours has been shown to be more effective. So, whenever possible, schedule homework and study time during daylight hours.
- Do homework in a designated area that is well lit, quiet, and supervised if needed.
- Avoid the time loss of an "in-house field trip" by having all necessary supplies readily available.
- Encourage students to use Post-It notes to mark where they left off reading, to write their own notes before they take a break, or as tabs to mark important information.
- A great tidbit is to utilize **"DEAD"** time. Driving in the car to appointments, games, shopping, traveling by bus or train, or waiting in a doctor's office is ideal for quick flash card or split-page note reviews.
- If your child is a "dawdler," be sure to have him or her work in your presence. The kitchen table is an excellent spot. Set goals with specific times attached to them (e.g., "Your math homework looks like it will take twenty minutes to complete. We'll set the timer. See if you can complete it before the timer goes off.") Play "Beat the Timer!"
- If your child's concentration wanders as he or she is trying to study, teach him or her the **"checkmark technique."** This involves keeping paper and pencil near him or her. Every time he or she catches him- or herself **NOT** concentrating, he or she puts a check on the paper. The very act of making that check gets him or her back to work. In the beginning, there will be many checkmarks, but after one to two weeks, concentration will improve dramatically.
- Steer students to use their best learning styles. Use quality strategies that reduce the quantity of time needed.
- Take small breaks periodically. "If you simply learn continuously your retention of the information you are trying to learn drops steadily. However just before and just after you take a short break your memory for an item is much better. Therefore, if you take

---

Figure 11.3 (continued)

short breaks at something like 30 to 60 minute intervals, you will find out you remember more. So, if you take time out while studying, the amount you will actually learn increases" (shorter study periods are needed for younger children; Recall Plus, 2004).

- During study breaks, stand—the body *needs a stretch*. Try one of the following:
    - Tell yourself what you learned.
    - Ask yourself, "What do I still feel insecure about?" Think about how you might study differently.
    - Plan fun breaks, preferably ones that involve laughter.
    - "Laughter, often a by-product of humor, reduces tension and pain, increases attention and memory, enhances respiration, lowers blood pressure, and improves circulation" (Winter, 2004).
- Do the worst first because it requires more time and energy. With this task out of the way, life is an open road for remaining homework. Developing the habit of doing the worst first reduces the possibility of procrastination. Remember, you don't have to like it—you just have to do it.
- Review information for a test just before you go to bed. Your brain works on it while you're sleeping to make the connections into long-term memory stronger.
- Avoid distracters such as the TV, your toys, the telephone, the refrigerator "calling you," and so forth.

(See Appendix for parent handout of this figure.)

Figure 11.4 Avoid Distractions

Illustration by Bruce Wasserman

FORMULA FOR READING A BOOK

The "Formula for Reading a Book" (see Figure 11.5) will help you determine how long it will take to read an assignment. This will help you estimate the time needed to complete the reading. Then, go back to your week-at-a-glance planner and fill in how many minutes you need to read each day to finish on time.

Figure 11.5 Formula for Reading Book

FORMULA FOR READING A BOOK

1. Read for six minutes.

2. Count the number of pages read in six minutes. _____pages

3. Multiply number of pages read by ten. _____pp/hour
   This number equals the number of
   pages read per hour.

4. Divide number of pages per hour _____hours
   into number of pages in book.

   pages per hour/pages in book $/\underline{}$

This equals the number of hours it takes to read your book.

5. Multiply number of hours it takes to read your _____minutes
   book by sixty.

This equals the number of minutes it takes to read your book.

6. Divide the number of minutes it will
   take you to read the book by the
   number of reading days available
   to determine the amount of time to
   be read per day.

   Reading days/Minutes $/\underline{}$ _____minutes/day

"Cramming is a way to forget rather than remember."

—Sprenger

"Dost thou love life, then do not squander time, for that's the stuff life is made of."

—Benjamin Franklin

"Even if you are on the right track, you'll get run over if you just sit there."

—Will Rogers

"The greater danger for most of us is not that our aim is too high and we miss it, but rather that it is too low and we reach it."

—Michelangelo

"Procrastination is the thief of time."

—Author unknown

SUMMARY OF KEY CONCEPTS IN THIS CHAPTER

- Manage your time.
- Use a weekly After School Calendar.
- A Week-at-a-Glance Homework Sheet increases school success.
- Improve planning with this Formula for Reading a Book.

12

Thinking About How We Study

Understanding the Path to Classroom Success

POWER OF METACOGNITION

Just as teachers reflect and evaluate the success of a unit, similarly, they need to stop and guide students in examining which study techniques work most successfully. High-achieving students profit from affirmation that their study techniques work. For students not working up to their potential, the problem may not be a lack of study strategies but other factors that enter the picture. The following are questions to ponder:

- Review student assessment of modality strengths (see Chapter 2). Are the strengths being maximized?
- Discover how different study techniques need to be used with different subjects and materials. Are adaptations being made accordingly?
- Identify strategies that *do not* work. Eliminate them! Note what strategies **do** work.
- Are assignments up to date so one doesn't get that awful feeling of falling behind? If not, what changes can be made?
- Are organizational systems effective in keeping all necessary materials together for efficient unit reviews/tests? How might they be improved?
- Recognize the cause and effect of not studying. What needs to be done *daily* to change patterns that are not working?
- When taking a test, what strategies are used that help you perform well? Are more tips and techniques needed in this area? See http://www.testtakingtips.com/ and www.charliefrench.com/ test_tips.htm.

Our goal is for students to learn that what works for their friends may not necessarily work best for them, as each has different strengths. The amount of time each student needs to spend studying will also vary. All students must know and value themselves as learners.

We recognize initial time spent modeling and practicing study strategies processes may add additional demands on teachers pressured to "cover" the curriculum. Today, teachers are driven by district test demands—local, state, and national. Given the demands of test pressures, teachers may feel that there is no time to guide students to reflect metacognitively on **how** they study and how they can improve studying. Yet the time devoted to developing good study strategies will provide a lifetime of payback for the students. Bear in mind this perspective:

> The greatest enemy of understanding is *coverage*. As long as you are determined to *cover* everything, you actually insure that most kids are not going to understand. You've got to take enough time to get kids deeply involved in something so they can think about it in lots of different ways and apply it . . . not just at school but at home and on the street and so on.

Or to state it more succinctly, "The best way to *cover* curriculum is to sit on it!" according to author and consultant Wanda Lincoln (1990). What we really want to do as teachers is *uncover* curriculum so students will understand.

SETTING GOALS AND CHOOSING SUCCESS

We would like to share the following activities as quick and easy ways to transfer the responsibility for studying onto students' shoulders. Begin the year by asking students to write goals using the "Choose Success" hand (see Appendix). Then throughout the year, guide students to self-evaluate study skills with "Study Skills Reflections" and follow up periodically with "How Am I Doing," both found in the Appendix. At report-card time, ask the students to decide if the grades received met the expectations they had set for themselves. If not, why not? Discuss what study habit changes may be needed. If expectations have been met or exceeded, reevaluate and set more challenging goals. Students with strong study strategies and habits will more easily take control of learning and be more successful in the educational world.

"Winners don't set limits—they set goals!"

STUDENTS WRITE REPORT CARD COMMENTS

Another self-evaluation technique is to ask students to write three or more comments that describe their academic progress, use of study strategies, and attitude and behavior. Request that they reflect honestly and carefully. Plan to use at least one of these comments on their report cards and tell pupils of your intent.

If computerized report cards and comment sheets are used, give students a copy of "Writing My Own Report Card" and ask them to circle the four most appropriate statements that describe their academic and behavioral progress (see Figure 12.1). On the back of the paper, explain why each comment was selected.

STUDYING TO BE A WINNER

After several years of working to embed study strategies into curriculum, the "Studying to Be a Winner" rubric was developed. It's both a roadmap, highlighting factors affecting studying, and an evaluative tool. Model and teach all the strategies in the "HOW" section of the rubric and coach students in using "WHEN" techniques. Then present the rubric to students, discussing and reflecting how various aspects are valuable in improving study habits.

Use this rubric with a unit test, or for quarterly evaluations. To evaluate performance on a test, ask students to complete the rubric and hand it in before taking the test or attach it to the end of the test. The rubric will validate grades for most students and provide a clear picture of what study methods make them a "winner" or what needs to be changed in preparing for future tests. Methods that **don't** work need to be eliminated.

No one wants to "just get by." An important aspect of real learning takes place when people immediately reflect on their performance. This debriefing will guide students in thinking about their study habits. Nothing drives home a message quicker than studying followed by the joy of high performance or the doldrums of poor performance precipitated by inadequate preparation.

ESTABLISH THE SELF-AFFIRMATION HABIT

We spoke about affirmation in Chapter 4. Now let's take the next step. As we strive to eliminate put-downs, it's equally important to learn to pat ourselves on the back with positive self-affirmations. All students must know and value themselves as learners. Teachers and parents need to model affirmations and encourage everyone to incorporate positive self-thoughts. Daily messages such as "I am good and getting better"; "I'm giving myself a round of applause"; or "Studying really paid off—I'm proud of my work" build confidence. Success breeds success!

Figure 12.1 "Writing My Own Report Card"

Report Card Comments

POSITIVE BEHAVIOR

1. Shows self-confidence in ability
2. Is a positive influence in class
3. Has a positive attitude
4. Is courteous and respectful
5. Is a very responsible student
6. Is enthusiastic and motivated
7. Super quarter—Keep up the good work
8. Is showing more self-control
9. Follows directions well

NEGATIVE BEHAVIOR

10. Lacks self-confidence in ability
11. Can be a disruptive influence
12. Is often inattentive in class
13. Lacks necessary social skills
14. Does not respect others' viewpoints
15. Is discourteous and disrespectful
16. Not eligible for a grade due to excessive absences
17. Does not follow safety rules
18. Shows little concern for grade
19. Poor music lesson attendance hindered grade
20. Did not fulfill reading workshop requirement

POSITIVE ACADEMIC

21. Is working on above-grade level material
22. Shows satisfactory progress
23. Shows good progress
24. Does consistently good work
25. Work has shown improvement
26. Work reflects creativity/imagination
27. Shows improvement in understanding
28. Expresses thoughts well in writing
29. Shows depth of knowledge in subject
30. Has a good understanding of concepts
31. Works well independently
32. Pursues extra projects independently
33. Does homework consistently
34. Does outstanding work
35. Actual grade is higher than grade given
36. Is working to potential
37. Commendable effort in all areas
38. Participates well in class discussion
39. Demonstrates high motivation
40. Assignments are thorough and complete
41. Demonstrates excellent work habits
42. Manages time and effort wisely
43. Hard worker
44. Fine job this quarter
45. Works hard, finds subject difficult
46. Works hard, has difficulty with tests
47. Seeks extra help when necessary
48. Shows improvement since 5-week report
49. Grade reflects work done on home instruction

NEGATIVE ACADEMIC

50. Did not fulfill journal/reading requirement
51. Should seek extra help
52. Poor laboratory grades
53. Passing grade but has ability to do better
54. In danger of failing for the year
55. Shows unsatisfactory progress
56. Needs to improve test/quiz grades
57. Needs to check work more carefully
58. Needs to improve listening skills
59. Needs to improve organizational skills
60. Needs to improve spelling
61. Is capable of better work
62. Shows weakness in vocabulary
63. Has difficulty with written expression
64. Has difficulty with course concepts
65. Has difficulty with following directions
66. Has a weak knowledge of number facts
67. A few low grades hurt average
68. Quarterly exam hurt average
69. Performance is inconsistent
70. Did not complete all required homework
71. Quality of homework needs improvement
72. Has not completed all required classwork
73. Quality of work is erratic
74. Is not working up to potential
75. Failed to complete assigned project(s)
76. Little/no effort since 5-week report
77. Effort is inconsistent
78. Needs to improve work/study habits
79. Exhibits minimal effort
80. Frequently comes to class unprepared
81. Does not submit assignments on time
82. Does not make up work missed when absent
83. Has difficulty with problem solving
84. Talking in class distracts from learning

GENERAL

85. Individualized marking system
86. Large number of days absent
87. Grade indicates mid-point average
88. Is frequently tardy
89. Has difficulty reading assigned material
90. Is a pleasure to have in class
91. Recommended for Technology sequence
92. Five-week report issued but not returned
93. Frequent absence hinders achievement
94. New entrant–no grade available
95. Participating in a modified program
96. Effort is satisfactory
97. Actual average is below grade given
98. Non-English speaking student— grade cannot be given
99. Recommended for Family/Consumer sequence

Name_____ Please *circle* two comments that describe your progress in learning and using study strategies that work for you. Then underline two comments that describe your achievement in class. Know that I will use at least one of your suggested comments. Please reflect honestly and carefully.

Figure 12.2 "Studying to be a Winner"

Circle the statements that describe your study strategies

	A Winner	In the Competition	May Get By	Just Getting By
WHEN	• Began studying 2–3 days before the test. • Studied 2 or more times a day for short periods of time.	• Studied the night before the test.	• Looked over information briefly just before the test.	• Just thought about it in class.
WHERE	• In a place where I could concentrate without distractions. • Your regular study area. • At the library.	• Any place I could find.	• On the school bus, or in the cafeteria, or during homeroom.	• Had difficulty finding a place to study.
HOW	• Gathered all study materials needed. • Used graphic organizers or drawings. • Used actions. • Made up songs with rhythm. • Used split-page notes or flash cards. • Put aside what I already knew & focused on what I had to learn. • Had someone quiz me. • Thought of tricks, mnemonics, or acronyms to remember difficult things. • Studied with a group. • Tape recorded information to review by listening. • Repeated writing of ideas or words. • Taught someone the information.	• Used two or three study techniques of a winner.	• Read over the notes or textbook.	• Relied only on information learned during class.
WHY	• It's fun! • To learn everything I can about the subject. • Knowing this information will make future learning easier. • To make my parents proud of me.	• To get a good grade. • To make the honor roll. • To make my parents proud of me.	• To pass the test. • So my parents won't yell at me.	• I can't think of a reason.

P-M-I

The **P-M-I**, which stands for plus, minus, interesting (A-ha moments) is a powerful, metacognitive tool for open-ended evaluation (see Appendix). It's successful with students at all levels and can be used for project, unit, and yearlong reflection. Students record positives (plusses) under **P**. In the **M** column (minuses), they list what was not valuable or important to them. The third column is for **I** (interesting) A-ha moments and items of high intrigue. When completed with integrity, it provides the teacher with a window into the minds and hearts of the students, as well as showing the effectiveness of teaching styles and strategies. Try it—you'll like it!

Sample PMI

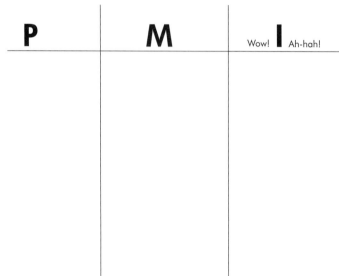

ABC'S OF SUCCESSFUL STUDY STRATEGIES

Generating an "ABC's of Successful Study Strategies" list during the last few months of school effectively crystallizes the myriad influences that effect students' memory and learning. Here's how you do it:

1. Ask students to write the letters A through Z down the far left margin of two pieces of notebook paper, skipping a line between each letter.

2. The students individually list successful study tips beside the appropriate alphabet letter. Write small and don't worry about spelling. This does not need to be done in alphabetical order—each letter is filled in as ideas occur. For example, **U**—underline important facts in your notes; **D**—draw a diagram.

3. Groups of two to four students now share their lists, assisting each other as each student records all the ideas given. If something is shared that anyone in the group doesn't understand, be sure clarification is given so all group members can explain it to the class.

4. Finally, the groups share as an entire class, again recording all ideas given as the teacher makes a master chart using correct spelling. Once more, clarify any ideas not understood by everyone.

Alternative Application

An ABC list is an effective way to review any unit, topic, or book. This activity can also be used as a preteaching device, to activate prior knowledge. Then after the unit is completed, add to the ABC list, using a different color, to record new knowledge.

Figure 12.3 ABC List

A Act out scenes about your subject Actively study	**N** Note-take using key words Name new vocabulary in the unit
B Believe you can master the subject **Bold** key words in the definitions	**O** Outline information in split-page format Omit practicing flash cards you know
C Circle key words in your notes Conduct a conversation about the topic	**P** Perform a silly routine to learn the topic Put new information to music
D Draw a diagram Do a daily review of your notes	**Q** Quiz yourself periodically as you read Quit and take a break every 30–60 minutes
E Explain as if you're teaching somone else Exaggerate and visualize	**R** Rap the information to remember it Review daily for 10 to 15 minutes
F Form a study group Find objects that symbolize the topic	**S** Set realistic goals Schedule laughter breaks
G Graphically organize your ideas Go over your notes just before bedtime	**T** Think positively! "Talk out" the information to be learned
H Have copies of all your study materials Highlight key words	**U** Understand your assignments Underline important facts in color
I Incorporate humor Image your notes	**V** Value yourself as a learner Visualize the events you're studying
J Jot down notes while you read Just say, "Yes! I can do it!"	**W** While taking notes, use abbreviations Write down all homework assignments
K Keep an eye on your study schedule Keep an idea journal on each subject	**X** X-ray information. Look at it from every angle X everything you already know & don't have to study
L List priorities Learn special vocabulary for each subject	**Y** You can do it! Believe that! Yummy non-fat yogurt is a brain-friendly snack
M Memorize with Mnemonics Mind map your knowledge	**Z** Zero-in on details that fascinate you Zoom to the head of the class!

"Practice does not make perfect. Practice makes permanent. However, perfect practice makes perfect."

—Sousa

"Some information must be over-learned to become permanent."

—Sprenger

"Luck is what happens when preparation meets opportunity."

—Elmer Letterman

"The harder you work the luckier you get."

—Gary Player, golfer

"Retrieved memories are the only evidence we have of learning."

—Sprenger

"Failure is not the worst thing in the world. The very worst is not to try."

—Author Unknown

"I will study and get ready and someday my chance will come."

—Abraham Lincoln

SUMMARY OF KEY CONCEPTS IN THIS CHAPTER

- Understand the power of metacognition.
- Set goals and choose success.
- Write report card comments.
- Studying to be a winner.
- Establish the self-affirmation habit.
- Use P-M-I (plus, minus, interesting) to evaluate.
- Utilize ABC's of successful study skills.

Appendix

"Phonics Phone"

1. To make your own phonics phone, the following materials are needed: a ten-foot length of PVC pipe, which needs to be cut into three inch pieces, and two three-fourths-inch diameter elbow PVC pipes per phone.

2. Put an elbow on either side of the pipe piece, and voila! You have a phonics phone. You will get approximately forty phone sections from each pipe length, and when two elbows are added to each three-inch piece of pipe, the cost is well under two dollars per phone.

3. They can be used from year to year—just disinfect them to reuse! Write each student's name on a phone with permanent magic markers, and at the end of the year, take it off with nail polish remover.

Figure 2.1   Phonics Phone

Illustration by Bruce Wasserman

How to Make a Floor Grid

1. Purchase the following materials:
   One ten-foot by twenty-foot heavy duty, clear plastic drop cloth
   Three rolls high-quality masking tape
   One roll of silver-gray, two-inch, nine-millimeter duct tape
   One roll of red, two-inch, nine millimeter duct tape

2. Find a floor covered with eight-inch square tiles which provides a "ready-made" measure for your grid. A pair of scissors is also needed.

3. Spread the drop cloth out on the eight-inch by eight-inch tiled floor and align one corner of the drop cloth with the right angle corner of any tile on the floor. Tape the plastic cloth to the floor to prevent shifting. Smooth out any wrinkles so the cloth lies flat and square over the tiled floor.

4. Using the tile lines as your guide, put down strips of masking tape over both horizontal and vertical floor tile lines.

5. Find the midpoint on the twenty-foot side of the drop cloth, put down the silver-gray, two-inch-wide duct tape. This marks the prime meridian, zero degrees longitude.

6. Then find the midpoint of the ten-foot side and put down the red, two-inch wide duct tape. This is the equator, zero degrees latitude. Since the equator has the most sunlight throughout the year, the red tape is used to mark this line.

7. Each masking tape line represents ten degrees. Label zero degrees longitude and latitude. You will have approximately 70 degrees north and south of the equator and 140 degrees east and west of the prime meridian. Remind students this grid does not surround the whole globe.

8. Place a compass rose above the northern hemisphere to show directions.

9. Carefully fold and place in a large plastic bag to store.

It will take two people approximately two hours to construct a plastic floor grid, but it will last for years of whole-body learning. Ask children to take off their shoes and step carefully when walking on the grid.

Other activities using the floor grid:
   Human bar or line graphs
   Walking integers on a number line
   Plus your creative ideas

Grid Over World Map

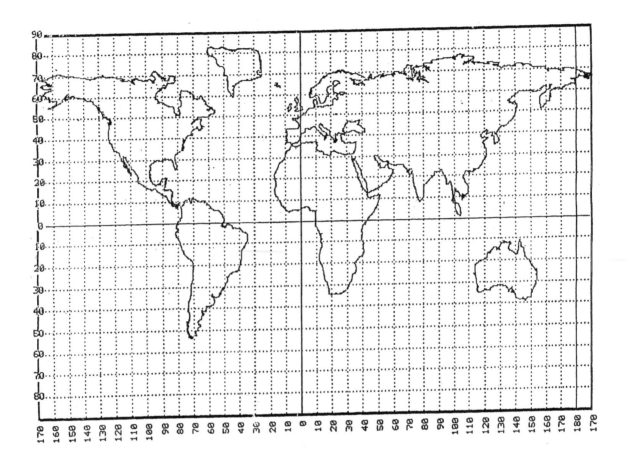

Yarn Map

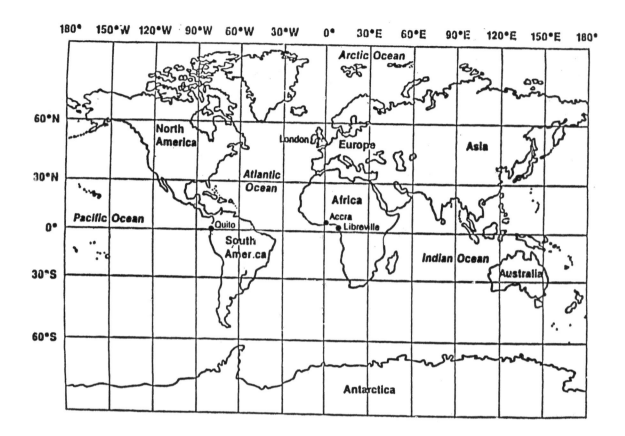

Study Map of Africa

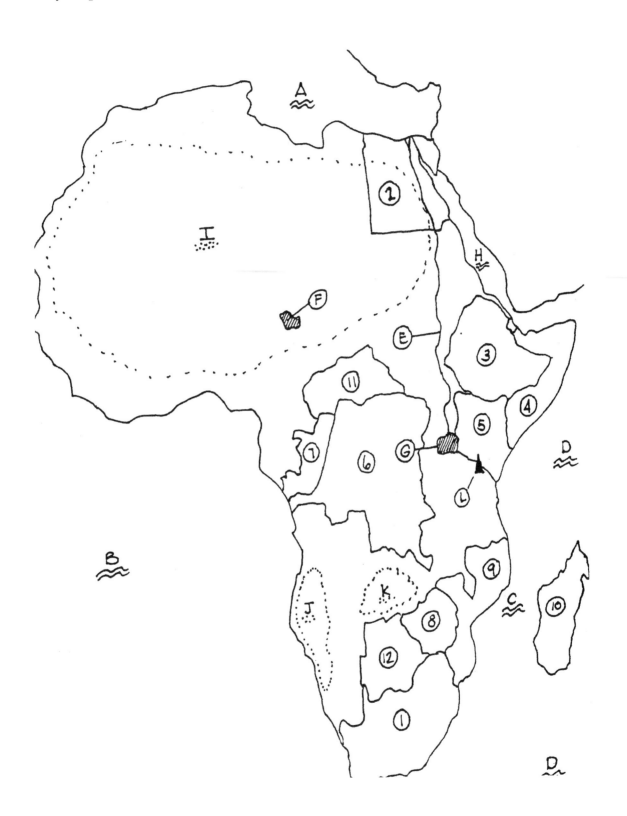

Bingo Board (with directions)

-Instruct students to write one term to be learned in each box. -Play "Bingo" with the teacher "calling the word meanings.		**Bingo Follow-up** -As homework, students draw a sketch to explain the meaning of the word printed on the front. Or -Write just <u>one key word</u> on the back of the card as a clue to the meaning.	
-Students cover their choice with a small square of paper. -When a student covers 4 boxes in a row, he/she calls out "Bingo!" -To be a winner, the student needs to say the word covered and give its meaning or explanation.	**Bingo Board** **Free Space**	-The next day students share their pictures or key words with a partner. -Play Bingo with the pictures or key words.	
		-Students cut boxes into flash cards for additional study.	

Bingo Board (blank)

	Bingo Board **Free Space**	

Fraction Cubes

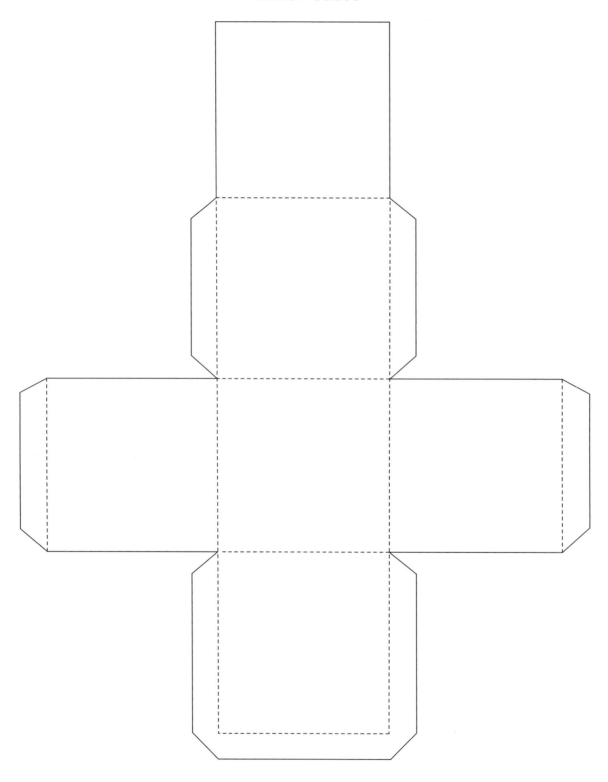

CHOOSE SUCCESS

Students are asked to trace their hands on construction paper. Next they cut out their hands and neatly print their names in the palm with a dark colored marker. On each finger they use a ballpoint pen to print one study skill that they personally need to use to be successful in school. Ideas are shared in small groups, such as:

- time management and organizational techniques
- specific studying ideas and things to do

These hands are put on the wall around the large black letters: CHOOSE SUCCESS!

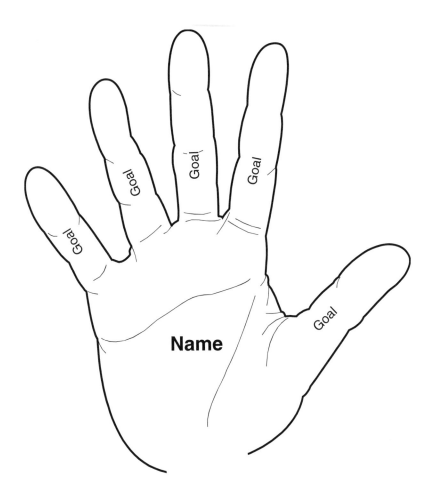

Credit: Janice Melichar-Utter

STUDY SKILL REFLECTIONS

We have reviewed many study skills in recent weeks. Our goal is for you to be successful in school and enjoy learning. Let's work together in setting some goals.

Sometimes we set "impossible" goals, like trying to get all "A's" or perfect attendance. Setting goals is not about being "the best" or about being perfect; it's simply a way to improve things in an organized way. When we set goals for ourselves, we need to break the whole thing into smaller steps. Each long journey begins with a single step! Keep this in mind.

1. What average would you like to aim for this quarter? _____

2. List the study strategies you need to carry out each day to attain this goal. Be specific. _____

_____

_____

_____

_____

_____

_____

_____

_____

_____

_____

_____

Student signature: _____

Parent signature: _____ Date:_____

HOW AM I DOING??

Reflect on what you have learned in this unit (or quarter) by listing three or more new things you learned in column one. In column two, explain what helped you to remember each idea.

<u>**Ideas Learned**</u>	<u>**How or Why I Remember It**</u>
1.	
2.	
3.	

Use the back if more space is needed.

****

Reflect on how succesfully you met your study skill goal.

_____

_____

_____

_____

What was your average this quarter? _____

Did you meet your goal?_____Why or Why Not?_____

_____

Thinking about the last quarter, write a new set of study skill goals for next quarter.

_____

_____

_____

_____

Student Signature:_____

Parent Signature:_____ Date_____

Strategies to Optimize Study

- Establish a consistent homework time within the constraints of the child's after school calendar. Work done during daylight hours has been shown to be more effective. So, whenever possible, schedule homework and study time during daylight hours.
- Do homework in a designated area that is well lit, quiet, and supervised if needed.
- Avoid the time loss of an "in-house field trip" by having all necessary supplies readily available.
- Encourage students to use Post-It notes to mark where they left off reading, to write their own notes before they take a break, or as tabs to mark important information.
- A great tidbit is to utilize **"DEAD"** time. Driving in the car to appointments, games, shopping, traveling by bus or train, or waiting in a doctor's office is ideal for quick flash card or split-page note reviews.
- If your child is a "dawdler," be sure to have him or her work in your presence. The kitchen table is an excellent spot. Set goals with specific times attached to them (e.g., "Your math homework looks like it will take twenty minutes to complete. We'll set the timer. See if you can complete it before the timer goes off." Play "Beat the Timer!").
- If your child's concentration wanders as he or she is trying to study, teach him or her the **"checkmark technique."** This involves keeping paper and pencil near him or her. Every time he or she catches him- or herself **NOT** concentrating, he or she puts a check on the paper. The very act of making that check gets him or her back to work. In the beginning, there will be many checkmarks, but after one to two weeks, concentration will improve dramatically.
- Steer students to use their best learning styles. Use quality strategies that reduce the quantity of time needed.
- Take small breaks periodically. "If you simply learn continuously your retention of the information you are trying to learn drops steadily. However just before and just after you take a short break your memory for an item is much better. Therefore, if you take short breaks at something like 30 to 60 minute intervals, you will find out you remember more. So, if you take time out while studying, the amount you will actually learn increases" (shorter study periods are needed for younger children; Recall Plus, 2004).
- During study breaks, stand—the body *needs a stretch*. Try one of the following:
    - –Tell yourself what you learned.
    - –Ask yourself, "What do I still feel insecure about?" Think about how you might study differently.
    - –Plan fun breaks, preferably ones that involve laughter.
    - –"Laughter, often a by-product of humor, reduces tension and pain, increases attention and memory, enhances respiration, lowers blood pressure, and improves circulation" (Winter, 2004).
- Do the worst first because it requires more time and energy. With this task out of the way, life is an open road for remaining homework. Developing the habit of doing the worst first reduces the possibility of procrastination. Remember, you don't have to like it—you just have to do it.
- Review information for a test just before you go to bed. Your brain works on it while you're sleeping to make the connections into long-term memory stronger.
- Avoid distracters such as the TV, your toys, the telephone, the refrigerator "calling you," and so forth.

Permission to copy for parent handout.

PMI

P	M	I
		Wow! **I** Ah-hah!

References

Amen, D. (2005). *Making a good brain great*. New York: Harmony Books.

Anderson, D. (1988). *What you can see you can be!* Marina Del Rey, CA: DeVorss & Company.

Armstrong, T. (2003). *The multiple intelligences of reading & writing; Making the words come alive*. Alexandria, VA: Association for Supervision & Curriculum Development.

Bach, R. (1970). *Jonathan Livingston Seagull*. London: Macmillan Publishing.

Back to school: Start smart! Support school success. (n.d.). *Scholastic family matters parent guides*. Retrieved October 12, 2005, from http://www.scholastic.com/familymatters/parenting

Barrett, S. (1992). *It's all in your head: A guide to understanding your brain and boosting your brain power*. Minneapolis, MN: Free Spirit Publishing.

Barsch, R. H. (1974). *Ray H. Barsch presents "...and sometimes y:" 109 fun ways to enjoy and improve spelling in the classroom*. Canogo Park, CA: The Ray Barsch Center for Learning.

Boggeman, S., Hoer, T., & Wallack, C. (1996). *Succeeding with multiple intelligences: Teaching through the personal intelligences*. St Louis, MO: The New City School.

Borgaard, M. (2005, January 20). *The period song*. Presented at Application of Multiple Intelligences and Study Skills workshop. Arlington Central School District, Arlington, NY.

Bragstad, B., & Stumpf, S. (1982). *A guidebook for teaching: study skills and motivation*. Boston: Allyn and Bacon.

Bushmiller, E. (1992, October 16). *Nancy cartoon*. Poughkeepsie Journal.

Cafarella, J. (n.d.). *Primacy-Recency effect*. Retrieved November 19, 2006, from sciencegnus.com/Primacy20%Recency.pdf.

Chan, A. S. (2003, July). Music training improves verbal but not visual memory. *Neuropsychology 17*(3).

Chapman, C. (1993). *If the shoe fits . . . How to develop multiple intelligences in the classroom*. Thousand Oaks, CA: Corwin Press.

Chapman, C. (2005). *Effective differentiated instructional strategies to maximize student learning*. Resource handbook. Bellevue, WA: Bureau of Education & Research

Chernin, F. (2004) *Learning styles: Cognitive preferences and learning styles: Leading with your Strength*. Toronto, Ontario, Canada: George Brown College. Retrieved October 4, 2006, from http://www.georgebrown.ca/saffairs/stusucc/learningstyles.aspx

Cherry, L. (1990). *The great kapok tree: A tale of the Amazon rain forest*. San Diego: Voyager Books.

Cohen, K. (n.d.). *The best kept secret of college success: Your # 1 asset*. Retrieved December 10, 2005, from http://www.associatedcontent.com/content.cfm?content_type=article&content_type_id=8266 Published September 10, 2005 by Karen Cohen.

Connecticut Parent Teacher Association. (2003). *Ten tips for fueling your child's brain power*. Retrieved October 12, 2005, from http://ctpta.org/parenting/brainpower.html.

Connell, J. D. (2005). *Brain-based strategies to reach every learner*. New York: Scholastic.

Costa, A. (1991). *The school as a home for the mind*. Thousand Oaks, CA: Corwin Press.

D'Arcangelo, M. (n.d.). *How can I create a brain-compatible classroom?* Retrieved October 4, 2006, from http://www.pnc.edu/ed/DeFoor/teach_your_children_well.htm

Dement, W., & Vaughan, C. (1999). *The promise of sleep.* New York: Delacorte.

Dennison, P., & Dennison, G. (1986). *Brain gym.* Ventura, CA: Edu-Kinesthetics, Inc.

Duckett, I., & Tatarkowski, M. (2005). *Practical strategies for learning and teaching on vocational programmes.* Retrieved October 6, 2006, from www.LSDA.org.uk

Dunn, R., Dunn, K., & Price, G. (1989). *Learning styles inventory.* Lawrence, KS: Price Systems.

Dunn, R., Griggs, S. A., Olsen, J., Gorman, B., & Beasley, M. (1995). A meta-analytical validation of the Dunn & Dunn learning styles model. *Journal of Educational Research,* 88(6), 353–361.

Dunnawind, S. (2003, September 20). Helping your kid get organized. *Times Herald-Record,* 3B.

Dusa G. (1992, July). *Using achievement to build self-esteem in your students* (Graduate course presentation). New York: Long Island University.

Ellis, D. (1997). *Becoming a master student.* Boston: Houghton Mifflin Company.

Feuerstein, R. (1990). *Instrumental enrichment.* Baltimore: University Park Press.

Fogarty, R. (1997). *Brain compatible classrooms.* Thousand Oaks, CA: Corwin Press.

Fogarty, R., & Stoehr, J. (1995). *Integrating curricula with multiple intelligences: Teams, themes, & threads.* Thousand Oaks, CA: Corwin Press.

Frender, G. (1990). *Learn to learn: Strengthening study skill and brain power.* Nashville, TN: Incentive Publications.

Gall, M. D., Gall, J. P., Jacobsen, D. R., & Bullock, T. L. (1990). *Tools for learning.* Alexandria, VA: Association for Supervision and Curriculum Development.

Gardner, H. (1983). *Frames of mind: The theory of multiple intelligences.* New York: Basic Books.

Glock, J., Wertz, S., & Meyer, M. (1999). *Naturalist intelligence—Science in the school yard.* Tucson, AZ: Zephyr Press.

Goldish, M. (2006) *Mnemonic songs for content area learning.* New York: Scholastic.

Goleman, D. (1995a). *Emotional intelligences: Why it can matter more than IQ.* New York: Bantam Books.

Growing Alberta. (2005). *Brain food.* Retrieved October 12, 2005, from http://www.growingalberta.com/parents/default.asp?id=350

Hanshumaker, J. (1980). The effects of arts education on intellectual & social development: A review of selected research. *Bulletin of the Council for Research in Music Education,* 61, 10–28.

Hart, L. (1983). *Human brain and human learning.* Oak Creek, AZ: Books for Educators.

Haynes, J. (2006, January/February). *Whatever works. Teaching PreK–8.*

Hegarty, M. *Fueled to Succeed.* Retrieved August 31, 2007, from http://content.scholastic.com/browse/article.jsp?id=1297

Highfield, R. (2006, January 24). The mind's enigma machine. *The Dana Foundation's Brain in the News,* 13, pp. 1–7.

Hornswaggled: These data do not exist. (n.d.). Retrieved October 18, 2006, from http://schoolof.info/infomancy/?p=230, www.developfaculty.com/tips/tip44.htm.

Jensen, E. (1995). *Super teaching.* Del Mar, CA: Turning Point Publishing.

Jensen, E. (1998). *Teaching with the brain in mind.* Alexandria, VA: Association for Supervision and Curriculum.

Jensen, E. (2000a). *Brain-based learning* (rev. ed.). Thousand Oaks, CA: Corwin Press.

Jensen, E. (2000b). *Learning with the body in mind.* Thousand Oaks, CA: Corwin Press.

Jensen, E. (2006, January). *IQ and BQ: How smart are you?* Presented at the Learning Brain Expo, San Diego, CA.

Johnson, D., Johnson, R., & Holubec, E. (1994). *Cooperative learning in the classroom.* Alexandria, VA: Association for Supervision and Curriculum.

Kagan, S. (1994). *Cooperative learning.* San Juan Capistrano, CA: Kagan Cooperative Learning.

Kettle, K., & Kagan, S. (2005). *Inspirational quotations.* San Clemente, CA: Kagan Publishing.

Lazear, D. (2004). *Higher order thinking the multiple intelligences way.* Chicago: Zephyr Press.

Levinson, H., & Sanders, A. (1992). *Turning around the upside-down kids: Helping dyslexic kids overcome their disorder.* New York: M. Evans and Company.

Lincoln, W. (1990). "Characteristics of Effective Teachers"; Presented at the Mid-Hudson Reading Council Fall Conference. Vassar College, Poughkeepsie, NY. October 11, 1989.

Lyle, V. (2006, January). *Strategies for bloomin' brains.* Presented at the Learning Brain Expo. San Diego, CA: The Brain Store.

Lyman, F., & McTighe, J. (1988). Cueing thinking in the classroom: The promise of theory-embedded tools. *Educational Leadership, 45*(7), 18–24.

Manning, M. (2002, May). *Visualizing when reading.* Teaching K–8. (89–90).

Markowitz, K., & Jensen, E. (1999). *The great memory book.* Thousand Oaks, CA: Corwin Press.

Marzano, R. J., Pickering, D. J., & Pollack, J. E. (2001) *Classroom instruction that works.* Alexandra, VA: Association for Supervision and Curriculum.

Math forum—Ask Dr. Math. (n.d.). *Finger multiplication for the 9s.* Retrieved February 13, 2005, from http://mathforum.org/library/drmath/view/59085.html

McCreery, J., & Hill, T. (2003, 2005, February). Illuminating the classroom environment [Electronic version]. *School Planning & Management.*

McGill, D. C. (1987, October 23). Painting saves a child. *The New York Times.*

McTaggart, J. (2005, October/November). *Using comics and graphic novels to encourage reluctant readers. Reading today.* Retrieved October 16, 2006, from http://www.thevirtualvine.com

Moretz, C. (2006). Planning with your students' brains in mind. In *Learning brain expo resource manual.* San Diego, CA: The Brain Store.

Mozart effect or not, music is good for the brain. (2004, July 18). *Poughkeepsie Journal.*

Music instruction aids verbal memory. (2003, July) *Neuropsychology.* Retrieved October 28, 2004, from http://www.eurekalert.org/pub_releases/2003-07/apa-mia072103.php

Nicholson-Nelson, K. (1998) *Developing students' multiple intelligences.* New York: Scholastic Professional Books.

Office of Teaching Effectiveness and Faculty Development. (2001, January). Brain-based learning 3—Nutrition for scholarly performance. *Nutshell Notes, 9*(1). Retrieved December 10, 2005, from http://www.isu.edu/ctl/nutshells/old_nutshells/9_1.htm.

Perkins, D. N. (Ed.). (1995). *Outsmarting I.Q: The emerging science of learnable intelligence.* New York: Free Press.

Poughkeepsie Journal. (2004, July 18). Mozart effect or not, music is good for the brain.

Pratt, S., & Matthews, K. (2004). *Fourteen foods that will change your life: Super food RX.* New York: William Morrow.

Prescott, J. O. (2005, January/ February). Music in the classroom: A user's guide for every teacher. *Scholastic Instructor, 29.*

Reardon, M. (2006). *Strategies for great teaching & learning.* Presented at the Learning Brain Expo, San Diego, CA.

Recall Plus (2004). *Study aids: Taking breaks at optimal times.* Retrieved October 6, 2006, from http://www.recallplus.com/breaks.asp

Redenbach, S. (2002). *Using the latest brain research to strengthen student learning: Practical classroom strategies that work (Grades 6–12).* Bellevue, WA: Bureau of Education & Research.

Roan, S. (2006, January 9). Faster, stronger, smarter [Special fitness issue]. *The Dana Foundation's Brain in the News*, 13, 1–8. Los Angeles Times newspaper of January 9, 2006, p. F4.

Robertson, D. (1985). *Blast off with book reports.* Carthage, IL: Good Apple.

Roger, S. (1999). *Teaching tips—105 ways to increase motivation and learning.* Evergreen, CO: Peak Learning Systems.

Sant, P. (2005, October 6). *Chi Kung exercise, swinging the arms.* Brewster, NY: American Center for Chinese Studies.

Seeger, P. (2000). Pete Seeger's Storytelling Book. New York, NY: Harcourt, Inc.

Severson, J. (2005). The principle of 10-24-7. In *Learning brain expo resource manual*, 2006. San Diego, CA: The Brain Store.

Silburg, J. (1998). *The I can't sing book: For grown ups who can't carry a tune in a paper bag. . . but want to do music with young children.* Beltsville, MD: Gryphon House.

Smith, A., Wise, D., & Lovatt, M. (2003). *Accelerated learning in the classroom.* Retrieved October 6, 2006, from http://www.highlandschools-virtualib.org.uk/ltt/flexible/accelerated.htm

Sorgen, M. (1997). *Strengthening student learning by applying the latest research on the brain to your classroom teaching.* Resource handbook. Bellevue, WA: Bureau of Education & Research.

Sousa, D. (2001). *How the brain learns.* Thousands Oaks, CA: Corwin Press.

Sprenger, M. (1999). *Learning & memory: The brain in action.* Bellevue, WA: Bureau of Education and Research.

Sprenger, M. (2002). *Becoming a "wiz" at brain-based teaching: How to make every year your best year.* Thousand Oaks, CA: Corwin Press.

Sprenger, M. (2003). *Differentiation through learning styles and memory.* Thousand Oaks, CA: Corwin Press.

Sprenger, M. (2005) *How to Teach so Students Remember.* Alexandria, VA Association for Supervision and Curriculum Development

Sprenger, M. (2006). Memory 101: You can always remember if you N.E.V.E.R. F.O.R.G.E.T. Presented at the *Learning Brain Expo*, San Diego, CA.

Squire, L., & Kandel, E. (1999). *Memory: From mind to molecules.* New York: Scientific American Library.

Sternberg, R., & Berg, C. (Eds.). (1992). *Intellectual development.* New York: Cambridge University Press.

Sylwester, R. (1995). *A celebration of neurons: An educator's guide to the human brain.* Alexandria, VA: Association for Supervision and Curriculum Development.

Tileston, D. (2004). *What every teacher should know about learning, memory, and the brain.* Thousand Oaks, CA: Corwin Press.

Trevine, J. (2001, March) Time line cadence. *Teaching K-8.*

Vurnakes, C. (1995). *The organized student: Teaching time management.* Torrance, CA: Frank Shaffer Publications.

Wallace, R. (1992). *Rappin' and rhymin': Raps, songs, cheers, and smart rope jingles for active learning.* Tucson, AZ: Zephyr Press.

Weaver, R., & Cortell, H. (1986). Using interactive images in the lecture hall. *Educational Horizons*, 64(4), 180–185.

Weinberger, N. M. (1998, November). The music in our minds. *Educational Leadership, 56,* 3.

William Glasser Institute. (n.d.) www.wglasser.com. Retrieved October 18, 2006, from http://www.greenspun.com.

Willis, M., & Hodson, V. (1999). *Discover your child's learning style.* Rosevilla, CA: Prima Publishing.

Wilson, M. A., & McNaughton, B. L. (1994). Reactivation of hippocampal ensemble memories during sleep. *Science, 265,* 676–670.

Winter, J. (2004, March/April) She Who Laughs Last. *Principal.*

Wolfe, P. (1991). Increasing Student Achievement by Applying the Latest Research on Memory and Learning. Bellevue, WA: Bureau of Education and Research.

Wolfe, P. (1998, November). Revisiting effective teaching. *Educational Leadership, 56,* 3.

Wolfe, P. (2001). *Brain matters: Translating research into classroom practice.* Alexandria, VA: Association for Supervision and Curriculum Development.

Wolfe, P. (2003). *The adolescent brain: A work in progress.* Retrieved September 13, 2006, from www.patwolfe.com/index.php?

Work-learning research. (2006). Retrieved October 18, 2006, from http://www.work-learning.com

Wormeli, R. (2005). *Summarization in any subject: 50 techniques to improve student learning.* Alexandra, VA: Association for Supervision and Curriculum Development.

Zull, J. E. (2002). T*he art of changing the brain—Enriching the practice of teaching by exploring the biology of learning.* Sterling, VA: Stylus Publishing.

Index

Dear Readers,

We would love to hear about the teacher-tested, brain-friendly study strategies you've developed. What unique applications have you created? How have they made a difference in your classroom? We will share them and happily credit your approach in future editions and workshops. Please include your name, address, e-mail address, and school. Readers and teachers in the future will appreciate your expertise.

Please send correspondence to either:

Amy Schwed
7 Panessa Drive
Poughkeepsie, NY 12603
amyschwed@optonline.net

Janice Melichar-Utter
7 William Way
Stormville, NY 12582
mrsjmutter98@aol.com

CURRICULUM MATERIALS
BALDWIN WALLACE UNIVERSITY

CENTRAL LIBRARY
TEESSIDE UNIVERSITY

CORWIN PRESS

The Corwin Press logo—a raven striding across an open book—represents the union of courage and learning. Corwin Press is committed to improving education for all learners by publishing books and other professional development resources for those serving the field of PreK–12 education. By providing practical, hands-on materials, Corwin Press continues to carry out the promise of its motto: **"Helping Educators Do Their Work Better."**